JAMESTOWN  EDUCATION

SIGNATURE READING

LEVEL E

McGraw Hill **Glencoe**

New York, New York   Columbus, Ohio   Chicago, Illinois   Peoria, Illinois   Woodland Hills, California

JAMESTOWN EDUCATION

Reviewers

Marsha Miller, Ed.D
Reading Specialist
Elgin High School
1200 Maroon Drive
Elgin, IL 60120

Kati Pearson
Orange County Public Schools
Literacy Coordinator
Carver Middle School
4500 West Columbia Street
Orlando, FL 32811

Lynda Pearson
Assistant Principal
Reading Specialist
Lied Middle School
5350 Tropical Parkway
Las Vegas, NV 89130

Suzanne Zweig
Reading Specialist/Consultant
Sullivan High School
6631 N. Bosworth
Chicago, IL 60626

Cover Image: Donald E. Carroll/Getty Images

Mc Graw Hill Glencoe

The *McGraw-Hill* Companies

ISBN: 0-07-861718-9 (Pupil's Edition)
ISBN: 0-07-861719-7 (Annotated Teacher's Edition)

Copyright © 2005 The McGraw-Hill Companies, Inc. All rights reserved. Except as permitted under the United States Copyright Act, no part of this publication may be reproduced or distributed in any form or by any means, or stored in a database or retrieval system, without prior written permission of the publisher.

Send all queries to:
Glencoe/McGraw-Hill
8787 Orion Place
Columbus, OH 43240-4027

2 3 4 5 6 7 8 9 113 09 08 07 06 05 04

Contents

How to Use This Book

Working Through the Lessons

The following descriptions will help you work your way through the lessons in this book.

Building Background will help you get ready to read. In this section you might begin a chart, discuss a question, or learn more about the topic of the selection.

Vocabulary Builder will help you start thinking about—and using—the selection vocabulary. You might draw a diagram and label it with vocabulary words, make a word map, match vocabulary words to their synonyms or antonyms, or use the words to predict what might happen in the selection.

Strategy Builder will introduce you to the strategy that you will use to read the selection. First you will read a definition of the strategy. Then you will see an example of how to use it. Often, you will be given ways to better organize or visualize what you will be reading.

Strategy Break will appear within the reading selection. It will show you how to apply the strategy you just learned to the first part of the selection.

Strategy Follow-up will ask you to apply the same strategy to the second part of the selection. Most of the time, you will work on your own to complete this section. Sometimes, however, you might work with a partner or a group of classmates.

Personal Checklist questions will ask you to rate how well you did in the lesson. When you finish totaling your score, you will enter it on the graphs on page 201.

Vocabulary Check will follow up on the work you did in the Vocabulary Builder. After you total your score, you will enter it on page 201.

Strategy Check will follow up on the strategy work that you did in the lesson. After you total your score, you will enter it on page 201.

Comprehension Check will check your understanding of the selection. After you total your score, you will enter it on page 201.

Extending will give ideas for activities that are related to the selection. Some activities will help you learn more about the topic of the selection. Others might ask you to respond to the selection by dramatizing, writing, or drawing something.

Resources such as books, recordings, videos, and Web sites will help you complete the Extending activities.

Graphing Your Progress

The information and graphs on pages 200–201 will help you track your progress as you work through this book. **Graph 1** will help you record your scores for the Personal Checklist and the Vocabulary, Strategy, and Comprehension Checks. **Graph 2** will help you track your overall progress across the book. You'll be able to see your areas of strength, as well as any areas that could use improvement. You and your teacher can discuss ways to work on those areas.

The Mystery in the Attic

Building Background

The story you are about to read is a mystery. A **mystery** always contains a kind of puzzle. The characters in a mystery use clues, or hints, to solve the puzzle. Think about a mystery that you have read or seen. What puzzle were the characters trying to solve? What clues helped them solve it? Get together with a partner and talk about your favorite mysteries. Then, on the concept map below, list several words or phrases that describe the characteristics of a mystery. Some examples are provided.

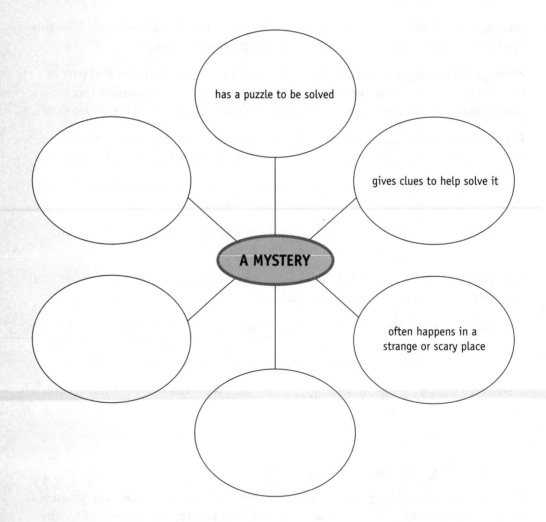

has a puzzle to be solved

gives clues to help solve it

A MYSTERY

often happens in a
strange or scary place

chimney

embezzling

faded

inspected

notepaper

regret

shivering

sunbeams

sundial

tiptoe

Vocabulary Builder

1. Some of the words in the margin are compound words. A **compound word** is made up of two words put together. Separating the words that make up a compound can help you figure out its meaning. For example, look at the words that make up *sundial*. Of course you know what the *sun* is, and you've seen a *dial* on a watch. A sundial has more in common with a watch than just its shape. Many years ago, a sundial was used to tell time. People figured out the time by measuring the shadow cast on the dial by the sun.

2. On the first clipboard, write the other vocabulary words that are compounds. Draw a line between the words that make up each compound. Use the words to figure out what the compound means.

3. On the second clipboard, list the words that are not compounds. Then, as you read "The Mystery in the Attic," use context clues to help you figure out any of the words you don't know. If context doesn't help, use a dictionary.

4. Save your work. You will use it again in the Vocabulary Check.

CLIPBOARD 1

Compound Words

sun/dial

Strategy Builder

Making Predictions While Reading a Mystery

- While you read a mystery, you probably try to **predict**, or guess, what will happen next. Like a detective, you use clues to help you make your predictions.

- The clues in a mystery are sometimes called context clues. **Context** is information that comes before or after a word or situation to help you understand it better.

- As you read "The Mystery in the Attic," you will stop twice to make predictions. At each Strategy Break, you will write down which context clues helped you make your predictions. Then, after you finish reading the story, you will look back at your predictions and check your detective work.

CLIPBOARD 2

Not Compound Words

The Mystery in the Attic

by Jeanne B. Hargett

See if you can use the clues that the author provides to help solve the mystery in the attic.

Staring at the ancient three-story house, I'd have changed places with just about anybody. It had turrets and bay windows and carvings as fancy as those on a fairy-tale castle. It had a **sundial** at one end of the garden and a fish pond at the other. Inside, we discovered that it also had peeling paint, mildew-stained walls, and a shortage of bathrooms.

"I love it," Mom said.

"I hate it," I said at the same instant.

Dad cleared his throat. "It was built almost a century ago. It'll be good for another hundred years when a few repairs are made."

My older brother, Greg, counted as he darted from doorway to doorway. "What a house—fifteen rooms if you include the attic. And maybe an extra room behind a secret panel, Molly. Bet I find it first!"

"Disappear this minute for all I care," I snapped. Was I the only one to **regret** leaving our snug home in the country?

But after moving in, I had to admit the old house wasn't so bad. I spent hours reading on its cushioned window seats. When Greg wasn't looking, I **inspected** every inch of carved wood. I even agreed to go to the third floor with him to explore the attic.

 Stop here for Strategy Break #1.

Strategy Break #1

1. What do you predict will happen next? _____

_____

2. Why do you think so? _____

_____

3. What clues from the story helped you make your prediction(s)? _____

_____

 Go on reading to see what happens.

Greg led the way up the stairs, carrying a flashlight. But when he pushed open the attic door, we stood blinking at early afternoon sunlight streaming through three windows.

"Some attic," Greg said. "If it had a floor everywhere we could roller-skate up here. Be careful to stay on those wooden beams, or you could crash into the rooms below." Stepping carefully, he went to raise a window. "Wow! We're as high as the moon. Come see how small the sundial looks from here."

"High places scare me, and you know it," I told him. "I'm not coming near a window." Instead I followed a bridge of creaky flooring till it ended at a **chimney**. I was standing on **tiptoe** to trace the chimney's exit through the roof when I saw the doll-sized trunk. It sat on a brick ledge. Layers of dust had woven a blanket over its rounded top.

"Greg, come here—I've found something!" I said. Both of us reached for it. The trunk slipped from our fingers and dust swirled around us. After our sneezing stopped, we crouched by the chimney to examine the doll clothes that had tumbled from the trunk. There were velvet jackets with tiny embroidered flowers, dresses of yellow satin trimmed with pearls, and beautifully made silk bonnets.

The trunk's lid had been lined with silk, too. Someone had cut a slit in the fabric and tucked in a thin sheet of **notepaper**.

I let Greg unfold the brittle paper. Then, squinting at the **faded** ink, I read aloud these words:

"September 5, 1921. I, Hannah Forbes, must grow up. Mama says life in a new place will help us forget our trouble. But I cannot bear taking Samantha, Angenetta, and Cynthia from this home where my mother also grew up. The dolls belonged first to her, and she agrees. I shall leave them . . .

resting under wooden rails,
sheltered when the cold wind wails,
hidden where the shadows flee
*and **sunbeams** mark their place at three."*

⬣ **Stop here for Strategy Break #2.**

Strategy Break #2

1. Do your earlier predictions match what happened? _____ Why or why not?

_____

_____

2. What do you predict will happen next? _____

_____

3. Why do you think so? _____

_____

4. What clues from the story helped you make your prediction(s)? _____

_____

_____

➡ **Go on reading to see what happens.**

My voice trembled and trailed off. What long-ago trouble had driven Hannah away? And how old was she then?

Greg interrupted my trance. "'Hidden where the shadows flee and sunbeams mark their place at three.' Molly, it's clear as anything. They're buried near the sundial!"

We found shovels in the garage and raced out to the yard. After an hour of digging produced no results, I asked, "But what about the wooden rails?"

"There probably was a fence here then. Who knows what changes have been made in so many years? Keep digging!"

Finally I told Greg I needed to take a break. There was someone I wanted to see. "Miss Jamison at the library knows everything," I said. "As soon as I clean up I'm going to ask if she can tell us about the Forbes family."

Greg snorted. "And leave me with the dirty work? Nothing doing. I'm coming, too."

Miss Jamison's information set me **shivering** in spite of the afternoon heat. Hannah's father had been the president of a local bank and had been convicted of **embezzling** thousands of dollars. Depending on which person you believed, he was either a shameless thief or a kind man too soft-hearted when folks needed money. Like me, Hannah was eleven when she had had to change homes. I was glad we didn't share the same reason.

"Those dolls simply have to be found, Greg," I said as we walked back to the house.

"Five blisters prove I've been trying," he grumbled.

"It's more important now," I insisted. "I'll help dig. Just give me time to put their clothes away in the trunk."

Greg agreed and came back to the attic with me to shut the window. I finished folding the clothes, then picked up the fragile note. In the bright sunlight I saw two faded ink strokes I'd missed before.

"Greg," I yelped, "it says, 'resting under wooden TRAILS.' These walkways are Hannah's wooden trails. The dolls are here!" I soon got hot and dusty again trying to look under the boards, but Greg sat quietly by a window. "Aren't you going to help look?" I asked.

He pointed to a patch of sunlight on the floor near the window. "I've been waiting," he said. "I told you the sundial had to be involved. Hannah looked at it out this window. How else did she know the sun touches here at three o'clock?"

As we lifted a loose plank in the sunlit spot, I didn't care who got credit for finding the bundle below.

The dolls' china faces were still rosy. Gently I touched one painted smile after another. Which was Samantha? Which Angenetta? Which Cynthia? It didn't matter. Somewhere, I was sure of it, Hannah was smiling, too. ●

Strategy Follow-up

Go back and look at the predictions that you wrote in this lesson. Do any of them match what actually happened in this story? Why or why not?

_____

_____

_____

_____

_____

_____

_____

_____

_____

_____

_____

_____

_____

✓Personal Checklist

Read each question and put a check (✓) in the correct box.

1. How well do you understand what happened in "The Mystery in the Attic"?
    - ☐ 3 (extremely well)
    - ☐ 2 (fairly well)
    - ☐ 1 (not well)

2. How well do you understand why Molly changed her mind about the house?
    - ☐ 3 (extremely well)
    - ☐ 2 (fairly well)
    - ☐ 1 (not well)

3. How many vocabulary words were you able to put on the appropriate clipboards?
    - ☐ 3 (7–10 words)
    - ☐ 2 (4–6 words)
    - ☐ 1 (0–3 words)

4. In Building Background you listed some of the characteristics of a mystery. How well were you able to use those characteristics to help you predict what might happen in this story?
    - ☐ 3 (extremely well)
    - ☐ 2 (fairly well)
    - ☐ 1 (not well)

5. How well were you able to use context clues to help you predict what might happen in this story?
    - ☐ 3 (extremely well)
    - ☐ 2 (fairly well)
    - ☐ 1 (not well)

Vocabulary Check

Look back at the work you did in the Vocabulary Builder. Then answer each question by circling the correct letter.

1. Which words did you write on the clipboard called Compound Words?
    a. notepaper, sunbeams, tiptoe
    b. embezzling, faded, inspected
    c. chimney, shivering, regret

2. Which word were you able to figure out by using the context clue "a shameless thief"?
    a. shivering
    b. inspected
    c. embezzling

3. At the beginning of the story, Molly regretted leaving her home in the country. What does *regret* mean?
    a. feel sad about
    b. feel happy about
    c. feel afraid about

4. In the context of this story, what does the compound word *tiptoe* mean?
    a. walking very lightly and quietly
    b. standing or walking on the tips of the toes
    c. poking at something with the tip of a toe

5. When her brother wasn't looking, Molly inspected every inch of the carved wood in the house. What does *inspected* mean?
    a. ignored completely
    b. examined carefully
    c. cleaned very well

Add the numbers that you just checked to get your total score. (For example, if you checked 3, 2, 3, 2, and 1, your total score would be 11.) Fill in your score here. Then turn to page 201 and transfer your score onto Graph 1.

► Personal
Vocabulary
Strategy
Comprehension
►TOTAL SCORE

Check your answers with your teacher. Give yourself 1 point for each correct answer, and fill in your Vocabulary score here. Then turn to page 201 and transfer your score onto Graph 1.

Personal
►Vocabulary
Strategy
Comprehension
TOTAL SCORE

Strategy Check

Look back at what you wrote at each Strategy Break. Then answer these questions:

1. At Strategy Break #1, if you predicted that the children would find a secret in the attic, which clue would have supported your prediction?

   a. the story's title, "The Mystery in the Attic"

   b. "What a house—fifteen rooms if you include the attic."

   c. When Greg wasn't looking, I inspected every inch of carved wood.

2. At Strategy Break #1, which prediction would *not* have fit the story?

   a. The children will be interested in what they find in the attic.

   b. Greg will try to keep Molly from the attic.

   c. The children will try to solve a mystery that they discover in the attic.

3. At Strategy Break #2, which prediction would have been best supported by the story's clues?

   a. The children will use the note to figure out where the dolls are hidden.

   b. The children will fold the note back up and put it back in the trunk.

   c. The children will throw the note away and continue searching the attic.

4. Which clue explains that the trunk had not been opened for many years?

   a. It sat on a brick ledge.

   b. Layers of dust had woven a blanket over it.

   c. The trunk's lid had been lined with silk, too.

5. Which clue suggests that the secret in the attic had to do with dolls?

   a. "Greg, come here—I've found something!"

   b. The trunk slipped from our fingers.

   c. We crouched . . . to examine the doll clothes.

Comprehension Check

Review the story if necessary. Then answer these questions:

1. At the beginning of the story, how do Molly and Greg feel about moving into a new house?

   a. They're both excited about it.

   b. Greg is unhappy, but Molly is excited.

   c. Molly is unhappy, but Greg is excited.

2. Why do Molly and Greg have to be careful when they explore the attic?

   a. It has a secret panel that leads to an extra room.

   b. It doesn't have a floor everywhere.

   c. Their parents had told them to stay away from it.

3. Who is Hannah Forbes?

   a. Greg's younger sister

   b. a girl who had lived in the house long ago

   c. the librarian who knows all about the town

4. Why does Molly feel a special bond with Hannah?

   a. Hannah was the same age as Molly when she moved out of her house.

   b. Hannah had a large doll collection, just as Molly does.

   c. Like Hannah, Molly left a secret treasure behind in her old house.

5. Why doesn't Greg help his sister look for the dolls in the attic?

   a. He doesn't like dolls, so he doesn't care about finding them.

   b. He still thinks the dolls are buried near the sundial in the yard.

   c. He's waiting for three o'clock to see where the sunbeams appear.

Check your answers with your teacher. Give yourself 1 point for each correct answer, and fill in your Strategy score here. Then turn to page 201 and transfer your score onto Graph 1.

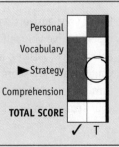

Personal

Vocabulary

▶ Strategy

Comprehension

TOTAL SCORE

✓ T

Check your answers with your teacher. Give yourself 1 point for each correct answer, and fill in your Comprehension score here. Then turn to page 201 and transfer your score onto Graph 1.

Personal

Vocabulary

Strategy

▶ Comprehension

TOTAL SCORE

✓ T

Extending

Choose one or more of these activities:

MAKE A SUNDIAL

By yourself or with a partner, make a sundial and use it to tell time. (See the book listed on this page for how to make the sundial.) Place the sundial outdoors and measure the angle of a shadow cast by the sun. Compare the time measured on the sundial with the time on a watch. How accurate is your sundial? Make adjustments if you need to.

CREATE CLUES FOR A TREASURE HUNT

Get together with a group of classmates and take turns hiding a "treasure." The person hiding the treasure should write clues to help the others find it. If you'd like, you can make the clues rhyme. For ideas, you can use the resources listed on this page or ones that you find yourself.

WRITE A MYSTERY

Write a mystery story about a secret in your home. The secret can be real or imaginary. Be sure your story contains some of the characteristics of a mystery that you listed in Building Background. If you'd like, ask some classmates to help you read your story aloud or perform it as a play.

Resources

Books

Lederer, Richard. *Pun and Games: Jokes, Riddles, Rhymes, Daffynitions, Tairy Fales, and More Wordplay for Kids.* Chicago Review Press, 1996.

Mayall, Newton, and Margaret Mayall. *Sundials: How to Know, Use and Make Them.* Sky Publications, 1973.

Sobol, Donald J. *Encyclopedia Brown: Boy Detective.* Skylark, 1985.

Web Sites

http://www.kudzukids.com
This site features a mystery that can be solved using the site's audio, video, and graphic files.

http://www.mysterynet.com
Search for "Kids Mysteries." This site presents a new mystery every week for kids to solve. It also offers a mystery-writing contest.

LESSON 2

Building Background

Some of the characters in "The Mystery of the Scythe" discuss events that took place during the Civil War. The Civil War began in 1861 and ended in 1865. The war greatly divided the people of the United States. People in the Southern states fought to keep their way of life. They split off from the Union and formed a new nation, the Confederate States of America. People in the Northern states fought to end slavery. They wanted to keep the Union together. Although the North won the war, it took many years for both sides to rebuild.

blade

clues

detectives

handle

mystery

rings

sapling

scythe

stump

Vocabulary Builder

1. Look up any words you don't know or can't pronounce. Then think about how some of the words are related, and put them into three groups. The first word in each group has been provided for you.

   Group 1: stump _____ _____

   Group 2: clues _____ _____

   Group 3: scythe _____ _____

2. Now write a sentence or two for each group of words. Be sure your sentences show your understanding of the words.

   _____

   _____

   _____

   _____

   _____

   _____

   _____

Strategy Builder

Following the Sequence of a Story

- When you read a story, you are reading a series of events. These events happen in order, or **sequence**. Paying attention to the sequence of events will help you: (1) follow what is happening, (2) predict what might happen next, and (3) make sense of the story.

- To make the sequence of events as clear as possible, authors often use **signal words**. Some examples of signal words are *first, next, before dinner,* and *later that evening.*

- The following paragraph is from a story about a girl named Anita. See if you can use the underlined signal words to follow the sequence of events.

> One morning Anita stood at the edge of a pool. She was afraid of the water and didn't want to learn how to swim. Suddenly the instructor told the children to get in. As they laughed and shouted, they jumped into the pool—all except Anita. Everyone watched and waited while she stood staring at the water. Finally she took a deep breath, held her nose, and jumped in. The children all cheered as she rose to the surface.

- If you wanted to track the order of events in the paragraph, you could put them on **sequence chain**. It would look like this:

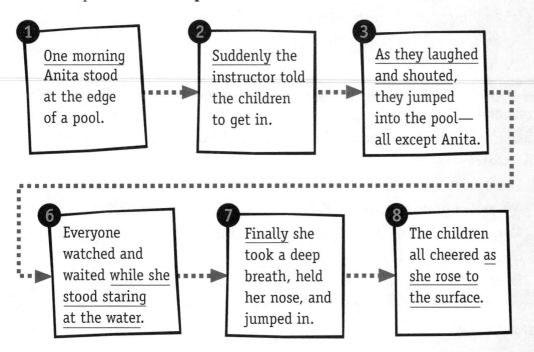

The Mystery of the Scythe

by Mat Rapacz

As you read the first part of this story, you can apply the strategies that you just learned. Notice the underlined signal words. They will give you a more exact picture of when things happened.

Billy Tubbs hated to see the big old oak tree come down. He had climbed its branches, hidden behind it while playing hide-and-seek, and escaped the sun's heat in its cool shade. But <u>now</u> the tree was dying, and Billy's mom and dad were afraid it would fall on their house.

Billy watched as the workmen climbed eighty feet into the tree and, with saws and ropes, began to take the old oak apart. "Acrobats with saws," his mother said.

<u>By late morning</u>, most of the tree was down, and a tall man with a chain saw began to cut through the three-foot-thick trunk. Billy got as close as he dared, mainly to look at the **rings**. His fifth-grade teacher, Mrs. Kelly, had told him that you could tell the age of a tree by counting the number of tree rings.

"Hey, Joe, there's a piece of metal stuck in here," the tall man called to his partner. "I almost cut through it."

Joe came over to take a look, and Billy moved closer. He watched as Joe used a handsaw and then a hammer and chisel to carefully free the object. It was a long, curved, rusty **blade**, obviously very old.

"It's a **scythe**," Joe said, holding it up.

"What's a scythe?" Billy asked.

"Well, boy," the tall man said, "this thing had a wooden **handle** at one time and was used to cut grass. Like this." He took the blade and made a side-armed motion with it. "How in the world did it get buried in the tree like that?"

"I'll bet it's been there over a hundred years," Joe said.

"Wow, a hundred years!" Billy was excited. "May I have it?"

"Sure, kid, it's your tree." The tall man handed the scythe to Billy. "Be careful with it."

Billy loved mysteries, and this was a good one: a scythe buried in an oak tree for over a hundred years. Who had put it there? And why? His parents might know.

Billy's father was still at work, but his mother thought it was a good **mystery**, too. "Somebody probably stuck it in when the tree was very young, and over the years the tree grew around it."

"Why, Mom? Why would somebody just leave it there?"

Mrs. Tubbs didn't know, but she had an idea. "Why not count the rings on the tree **stump** and figure out how long the scythe has been there?" Together, they went to the stump and counted. It was hard work. The stump was thick, and it was sometimes difficult to tell just where a ring started and ended. They <u>finally</u> decided that the tree was about 145 years old.

"Yikes!" Billy's dad said <u>when he got home</u>. "One hundred and forty-five years old? Are you sure?"

"Why not?" Mrs. Tubbs said. "Many oaks live two hundred years and more."

"What about the scythe, Dad?" asked Billy. "Why was it stuck in the tree in the first place?"

"I don't know," said Mr. Tubbs, "but we might be able to discover who put it there."

"How?" asked Billy.

"We have deeds to this property in our strongbox in the cellar. One of the old ones should tell us who owned the property when the oak was young. Maybe that's the person who stuck the scythe in the tree."

Billy and his dad got out all the old deeds. Each deed told who had owned the property and when. Billy and his father discovered that a man named James Bartow had owned it from 1850 to 1885.

"I guess that solves the mystery, Billy," said his dad. "James Bartow probably put the scythe there when the tree was small."

Billy wasn't satisfied. "But why, Dad?"

"Maybe just to see if the tree would grow around it." Mr. Tubbs thought for a minute. "The family owned the land during the Civil War. Maybe we can check some old records to see if a Bartow was a soldier."

"What good will that do?" Billy was puzzled.

"Maybe no good, but the more we learn about the family, the better chance we have of solving the mystery. Good **detectives** gather all the **clues** they can," his dad said.

<u>The next day</u> Billy and his father went to the library. Mr. Hogan, the librarian, found a list of all Hillman, New York, residents who had been soldiers during the Civil War. A John Bartow of the Fourteenth Regiment was listed as missing in action in 1864.

Billy and his father were learning things about the Bartow family, but they were no closer to solving the mystery. They decided to see if they could find any Bartow gravestones in the cemetery. The caretaker led them to an old section where most of the gravestones were worn and difficult to read.

They found three Bartows. James Bartow was born in 1821 and died in 1886. His wife, Amanda, was born in 1827 and died in 1878. Their son Charles was born in 1845 and died in 1922. There was no stone for John, the Civil War soldier.

There seemed little more they could do. Billy thought of looking in the telephone book for people named Bartow. None were listed for Hillman or nearby towns. "A good idea anyway," Mr. Tubbs said.

Stop here for the Strategy Break.

Strategy Break

Many things have happened in this story so far. If you were to create a sequence chain to put the main events in order, it might look like this:

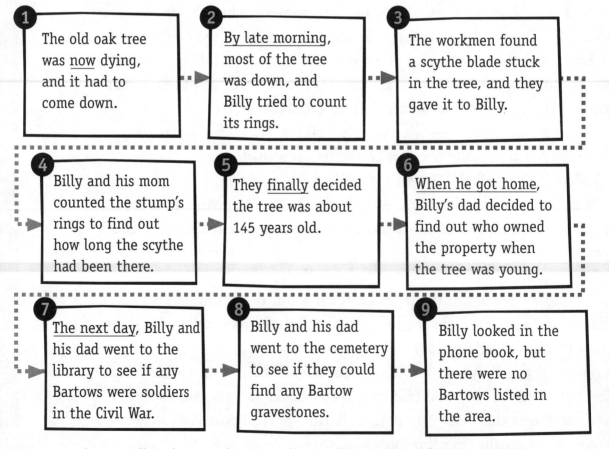

1 The old oak tree was <u>now</u> dying, and it had to come down.

2 <u>By late morning</u>, most of the tree was down, and Billy tried to count its rings.

3 The workmen found a scythe blade stuck in the tree, and they gave it to Billy.

4 Billy and his mom counted the stump's rings to find out how long the scythe had been there.

5 They <u>finally</u> decided the tree was about 145 years old.

6 <u>When he got home</u>, Billy's dad decided to find out who owned the property when the tree was young.

7 <u>The next day</u>, Billy and his dad went to the library to see if any Bartows were soldiers in the Civil War.

8 Billy and his dad went to the cemetery to see if they could find any Bartow gravestones.

9 Billy looked in the phone book, but there were no Bartows listed in the area.

As you continue reading, keep paying attention to the sequence of events. Also keep looking for signal words. At the end of this story, you will use some of them as you complete the sequence chain on your own.

➡ Go on reading to see what happens.

That night at supper, Billy's mom had one final idea. "If Charles Bartow died in 1922, there might be somebody still alive in Hillman who knew him. Charles may have told someone the story of the scythe."

The three of them made a list of the older citizens they knew in Hillman. On Sunday they set out to talk to them. Mrs. Weiss, the first on their list, remembered Charles Bartow but never talked to him. The second person, Mrs. Bradshaw, came to Hillman in 1923, the year after Charles Bartow died. Billy thought about quitting, but his mom reminded him that good detectives never give up.

Mr. Densky, who used to own a shoe store, was the third person on the list. He was almost ninety years old, and when Billy told him about the scythe and the Bartow family, Mr. Densky smiled and nodded his head.

"I didn't know old Charlie very well, but I know the story of the scythe. When I was about your age, young man, my father hitched up our horse and wagon and took me to see that scythe. When we got there—it was the Medford place then—my father showed me the end of the blade sticking out of the tree.

"He told me that when news of the Civil War reached Hillman, John Bartow was out cutting grass with his scythe. He immediately stopped work, hung the scythe in a little oak tree near the house, and told his parents, 'I'm going to join the army. Leave my scythe hanging in the tree until I return.'

"Three years passed. Then a letter came from an officer in John's regiment. After a fierce battle, John was missing, probably killed. The Bartows hoped that he had been taken prisoner, but when the war ended in 1865, John didn't return home. The scythe stayed in the tree, waiting for him.

"Over the years the **sapling** grew into a large tree," Mr. Densky continued, "and the wood began to grow around the scythe itself. Till the day they died, Mr. and Mrs. Bartow never gave up hope for John's return. And so the scythe remained. Gradually the handle rotted away until only the blade was left, and most of that had already been swallowed by the time I saw it. So that old scythe was in the oak tree more than 130 years, just waiting for John Bartow to return and pull it out.

"Everybody in Hillman knew that story back when I was a boy. Now I guess almost nobody knows it. Nobody remembers."

"Three more people remember now, Mr. Densky," Billy said.

Although he was sad for the soldier, Billy was glad the mystery was solved. He took the scythe blade to school and told his teacher and class about it. Mrs. Kelly put the scythe on display in a glass case with the story next to it. Now people would always remember John Bartow, the soldier who never returned. ●

Strategy Follow-up

Now complete this sequence chain for the second part of "The Mystery of the Scythe." It begins with event 10. Some of the chain has been filled in for you.

10 That night at supper,

11 On Sunday they talked to

12 Mr. Densky told them

13 Billy

14 Mrs. Kelly

15 Now

✓ Personal Checklist

Read each question and put a check (✓) in the correct box.

1. How well do you understand what happened in "The Mystery of the Scythe"?
   - ☐ 3 (extremely well)
   - ☐ 2 (fairly well)
   - ☐ 1 (not well)

2. How well do you understand the importance of the scythe to the Bartow family?
   - ☐ 3 (extremely well)
   - ☐ 2 (fairly well)
   - ☐ 1 (not well)

3. After reading the information in Building Background, how well were you able to understand why John Bartow left his family?
   - ☐ 3 (extremely well)
   - ☐ 2 (fairly well)
   - ☐ 1 (not well)

4. In the Vocabulary Builder, how well were you able to put the words into three groups?
   - ☐ 3 (extremely well)
   - ☐ 2 (fairly well)
   - ☐ 1 (not well)

5. How well were you able to complete the sequence chain in the Strategy Follow-up?
   - ☐ 3 (extremely well)
   - ☐ 2 (fairly well)
   - ☐ 1 (not well)

Vocabulary Check

Look back at the work you did in the Vocabulary Builder. Then answer each question by circling the correct letter.

1. Which words belong in the same group with *stump*?
   a. *rings* and *sapling*
   b. *mystery* and *detective*
   c. *handle* and *blade*

2. Which words belong in the same group with *clue*?
   a. *blade* and *scythe*
   b. *sapling* and *stump*
   c. *detective* and *mystery*

3. The sapling in which John hung his scythe grew into a large tree. What is a sapling?
   a. a tool used to cut grass
   b. a tree trunk
   c. a young tree

4. Which meaning of the word *rings* fits this selection?
   a. jewelry worn on the fingers
   b. round marks formed on a tree trunk
   c. the sounds made by a bell

5. Billy's parents keep encouraging him to be a good detective. What makes a good detective?
   a. A good detective gathers clues until the mystery is solved.
   b. A good detective doesn't ask very many questions.
   c. A good detective gives up when a problem gets hard.

Add the numbers that you just checked to get your Personal Checklist score. Fill in your score here. Then turn to page 201 and transfer your score onto Graph 1.

Personal	
Vocabulary	
Strategy	
Comprehension	
TOTAL SCORE	
	✓ T

Check your answers with your teacher. Give yourself 1 point for each correct answer, and fill in your Vocabulary score here. Then turn to page 201 and transfer your score onto Graph 1.

Personal	
Vocabulary	
Strategy	
Comprehension	
TOTAL SCORE	
	✓ T

Strategy Check

Review the sequence chain that you completed in the Strategy Follow-up. Then answer these questions:

1. What do Billy and his family do on Sunday?
    a. They talk to the workmen.
    b. They talk to Mr. Hogan the librarian.
    c. They talk to Mrs. Weiss, Mrs. Bradshaw, and Mr. Densky.

2. What does Mr. Densky tell Billy and his family?
    a. that he didn't know Charles Bartow
    b. the story of the scythe
    c. what caused the Civil War

3. Which of the following is *not* an example of signal words?
    a. Mr. Densky told them
    b. that night at supper
    c. on Sunday

4. What happens after Billy takes the scythe blade to school?
    a. Mrs. Kelly tells him to take it home.
    b. Mrs. Kelly puts it on display.
    c. John Bartow visits the school.

5. Which sentence tells the main events of this story?
    a. Billy and his mother cut down a tree, and then they meet some of the older citizens of Hillman.
    b. Billy and his father visit the library, the cemetery, and some of the older citizens of Hillman.
    c. Some workers find a scythe blade in a tree, and the Tubbs family tries to find out how it got there.

Comprehension Check

Review the story if necessary. Then answer these questions:

1. What do the workmen find when they cut through the trunk of the oak tree?
    a. an old wooden handle
    b. the rusty blade of a scythe
    c. a hammer and chisel

2. Why isn't Billy satisfied after learning who had probably put the scythe in the tree?
    a. He wants to find out why the person put it there.
    b. He wants to find out when the person put it there.
    c. He wants to find out how the person put it there.

3. What did John Bartow do when he heard news of the Civil War?
    a. He cut down the oak tree.
    b. He left home to join the army.
    c. He left home to open a shoe store.

4. Why did Mr. and Mrs. Bartow leave the scythe in the tree?
    a. They forgot that the scythe was in the tree.
    b. They weren't strong enough to remove it themselves.
    c. They hoped their son would return and remove it himself.

5. Why does Mrs. Kelly display the scythe blade in a glass case?
    a. She wants Billy to tell the class about the scythe.
    b. She wants Billy to forget about the scythe.
    c. She wants people to remember John Bartow.

Check your answers with your teacher. Give yourself 1 point for each correct answer, and fill in your Strategy score here. Then turn to page 201 and transfer your score onto Graph 1.

Personal
Vocabulary
Strategy
Comprehension
TOTAL SCORE
✓ T

Check your answers with your teacher. Give yourself 1 point for each correct answer, and fill in your Comprehension score here. Then turn to page 201 and transfer your score onto Graph 1.

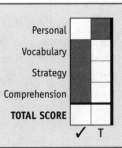

Personal
Vocabulary
Strategy
Comprehension
TOTAL SCORE
✓ T

Extending

Choose one or both of these activities:

RECORD FAMILY STORIES

Interview older family members about their experiences. They might tell you about historical events that they lived through. Or they might tell you about something special that happened to them. If you can, record your interviews on audiotape or videotape. Be sure to ask permission before you share the tapes with the class.

LEARN MORE ABOUT THE CIVIL WAR

Learn more about the Civil War by reading a book or watching a video. Share what you learn in one or more of the following ways:

- draw or paint a picture

- draw a map

- make a sculpture

- make a diorama

- act out a scene

Resources

Book

Dolan, Edward F. *The American Civil War: A House Divided.* Millbrook Press, 1997.

Web Sites

http://www.arborday.org/programs/teachingyouth.html
This site has a variety of games and activities that teach kids about trees.

http://www.hometown.aol.com/gordonkwok/cwpoetry.html
This site has many Civil War–era poems by famous poets as well as by soldiers, relatives, and others personally affected by the war. Each poem includes a brief introduction.

Bamboo Can Do!

Building Background

In this selection, you will learn why bamboo is used to build homes. Maybe you've never seen a bamboo building, but you've seen buildings made of other materials. Think about the buildings in your neighborhood. What are they made of? Brick, plaster, and wood are some common building materials. What are the advantages of each building material? What are the disadvantages?

buckle

collapsed

drawbacks

hollow

lashed

machete

rots

rubble

Vocabulary Builder

1. Like most words, the vocabulary words in the margin have antonyms and synonyms. **Antonyms** are words with opposite meanings. **Synonyms** are words with similar meanings. Knowing a word's antonym or synonym can help you learn and remember the word.

2. Circle the antonym of each boldfaced word. Use a dictionary if you need help.

collapsed	stood	fell
drawbacks	benefits	disadvantages
rots	decays	grows
hollow	filled	empty

3. Circle the synonym of each boldfaced word. Again, use a dictionary if necessary.

lashed	cut	tied
machete	knife	scissors
rubble	wreckage	building
buckle	stretch	bend

4. Save your work. You will use it again in the Vocabulary Check.

Strategy Builder

How to Read an Informational Article

- An **informational article** gives facts and information about a particular subject, or topic. The **topic** of an article is what the article is all about. The topic is often mentioned in the **title** of the article. For example, "Bamboo Can Do!" is about bamboo and why it is used to build homes.

- Most information articles are organized into **main ideas** and **supporting details**. These ideas and details help explain or support the topic.

- The main ideas are often stated in **headings** throughout the article. The supporting details are given in the paragraphs below the headings. The following example is from an informational article about German shepherd dogs. The supporting details are underlined.

German Shepherd Dogs

German Shepherds Make Good Work Dogs

German shepherds have many qualities that make them good work dogs. For one thing, they <u>are the right size</u>. They are quite large, which makes them strong. And with their big chests, they can get enough wind for long runs. They also <u>have a thick coat of fur</u> that protects them in bad weather and helps them stay clean. They <u>are very alert and smart</u>, so they are easy to train. And they <u>are calm and gentle</u>, which makes them patient with their owners.

- If you wanted to highlight the topic, main idea, and supporting details in the example above, you could put them on a **concept map**, or web. It would look like this:

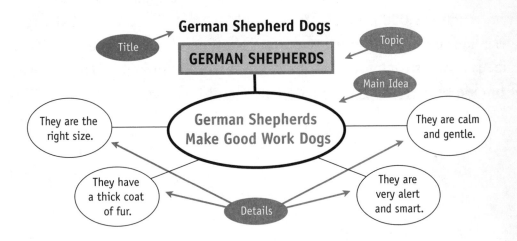

Bamboo Can Do!

As you read the beginning of this informational article, you can apply some of the strategies that you just learned. Notice the underlined phrases and sentences. They contain details that support the main idea in each heading.

Have you ever thought of building a home out of bamboo?

What can you do with bamboo? That's not a good question. A better question is, *What can't you do with bamboo?*

Bamboo is a tall, treelike grass. There are 350 different kinds of bamboo. Most grow in Asia. A few, though, are found in the United States.

Bamboo comes in handy for all sorts of things. It can be cut up and eaten. It can be used to make fishing poles or paper. Some people weave thin strips of it into mats or chair seats. They make curtains and chopsticks out of it. Bamboo stems can even serve as water pipes.

Super Strong

Bamboo is most amazing, though, when it is used in building. <u>Ounce for ounce, bamboo is much stronger than wood.</u> <u>It is much stronger than brick or concrete or steel</u>. If you don't believe that, think about what happened in Costa Rica.

In April, 1991, a big earthquake struck Costa Rica. One area was hit hard. Houses and hotels **collapsed** like piles of matchsticks. Heaps of concrete lay everywhere. In the center of the **rubble** stood 20 homes. They were made of bamboo. <u>Not one of the bamboo homes was damaged</u>. Not one even had a crack.

It's hard to understand just how strong bamboo is. But here's one way to do it. Picture a short, straight bamboo column. The surface area at the top is about the size of a playing card. Now picture an elephant. Let's say Jumbo weighs 11,000 pounds. What would happen if you could balance the elephant on top of the tiny column? Nothing! Bamboo is tube shaped. A tube is a very strong form, so the column would not bend. <u>Bamboo will not **buckle** or break—even under an elephant</u>! Isn't *that* strong?

A Real Bargain

Bamboo is not just strong; it's also cheap. The Costa Rican homes were built for about $4,500 each. There are reasons why bamboo costs so little. For one thing, <u>it grows fast</u>. A stalk of bamboo can grow <u>up to three feet per day</u>! So bamboo <u>can be used after only one year of growth</u>. A tree needs to grow for 20 years before it's ready to be used.

Another thing that makes bamboo inexpensive is that it is <u>easy to cut</u>. A hacksaw or **machete** will do the job. And once cut down, bamboo is light enough that it <u>can be carried away by the work crew</u>.

Bamboo is also a bargain because it's <u>simple to use</u>. No machines, no heavy trucks, no sawmill, no steel mill—just ready-to-use bamboo. No brick making and baking, no concrete mixing—just nice, clean, nonpolluting bamboo.

⬣ **Stop here for the Strategy Break.**

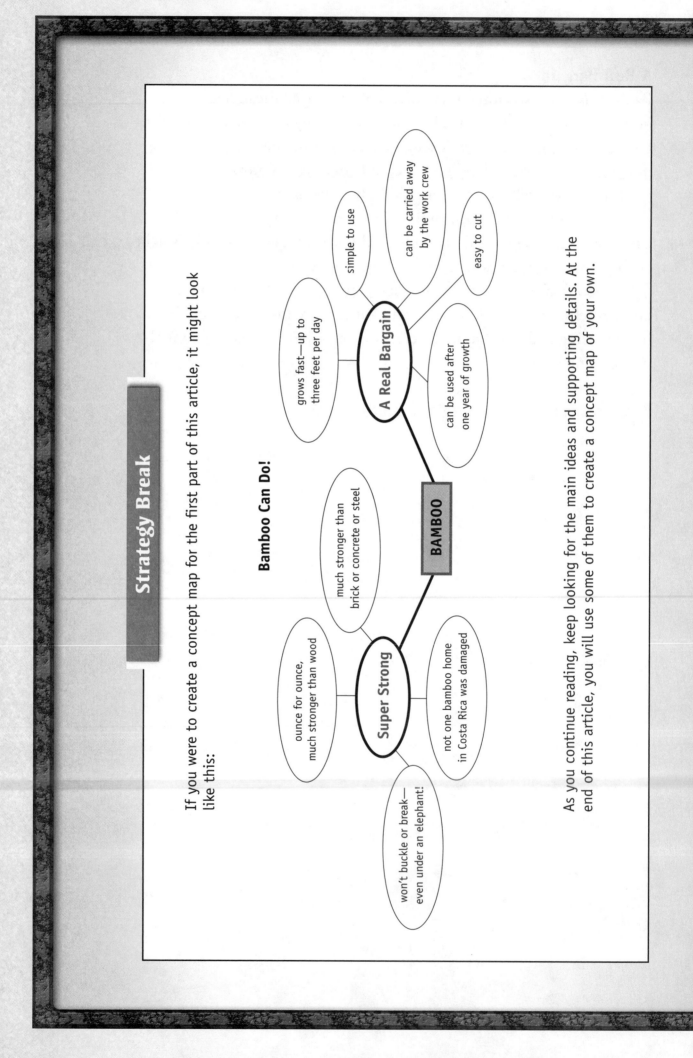

Strategy Break

If you were to create a concept map for the first part of this article, it might look like this:

Bamboo Can Do!

BAMBOO

A Real Bargain
- grows fast—up to three feet per day
- simple to use
- can be carried away by the work crew
- easy to cut
- can be used after one year of growth

Super Strong
- much stronger than brick or concrete or steel
- ounce for ounce, much stronger than wood
- not one bamboo home in Costa Rica was damaged
- won't buckle or break—even under an elephant!

As you continue reading, keep looking for the main ideas and supporting details. At the end of this article, you will use some of them to create a concept map of your own.

Go on reading.

Coming into Fashion

A well-made bamboo home will last 30 years or more. So why don't more builders use bamboo? In fact, more builders are interested in using it. Costa Rica has a special program. It is called the National Bamboo Project. It will build 1,000 bamboo homes per year. Other countries, in Asia and Africa, are watching the Costa Rican work.

Some Drawbacks

So, you may ask, why isn't every building a bamboo building? Bamboo has some bad **drawbacks**. It burns easily and fast. It is **hollow**, so the air inside each stalk feeds a fire.

The danger of fire means that bamboo should not be used for big buildings. Nor should it be used for multistory homes. The safest bamboo homes are only one story high. They have many windows and doors. If a bamboo home catches fire, the people inside must be able to get out fast.

Other Problems

Bugs are a big problem. For example, termites love bamboo. Beetles love it too. These bugs will eat right through a bamboo home. To prevent that from happening, the bamboo must first be soaked in a special liquid.

Water is also bad news because wet bamboo **rots** quickly. Within weeks, a damp bamboo house will fall apart. A bamboo house should have a big, wide roof. That way, even if it rains the walls of the house can stay dry.

A final problem is how to put bamboo together. Workers can nail wood and weld steel. They can use mortar for bricks. But how do they connect pieces of bamboo? In the past, people **lashed** bamboo poles together. Today, builders have a new method. They stick pieces of wood into the ends of the bamboo poles. Then they nail or glue the pieces of wood together.

Is Bamboo for You?

Bamboo houses have been around for a long time. In the past, only the poor used bamboo. Richer people thought wood and bricks were better. But engineers have studied bamboo. They have learned about its strength and other good qualities. The old ideas about bamboo are starting to change.

It's true that bamboo homes may never make sense in cold climates. A bamboo apartment building doesn't make sense either. But in the right place, for the right use, building with bamboo is a very smart idea. ●

Strategy Follow-up

Now create a concept map for the section of this article called "Other Problems." The topic, title, and main idea have been filled in for you.

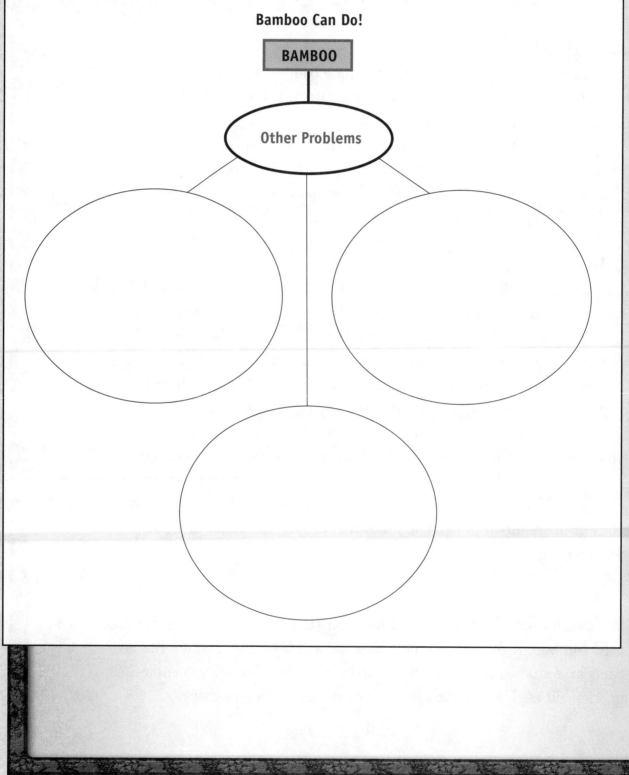

Bamboo Can Do!

BAMBOO

Other Problems

✓Personal Checklist

Read each question and put a check (✓) in the correct box.

1. How well could you explain the information in this article to another person?
   - ☐ 3 (extremely well)
   - ☐ 2 (fairly well)
   - ☐ 1 (not well)

2. How well do you understand why building with bamboo makes sense in some places but not in others?
   - ☐ 3 (extremely well)
   - ☐ 2 (fairly well)
   - ☐ 1 (not well)

3. After reading Building Background, how well were you able to understand that all building materials have both advantages and disadvantages?
   - ☐ 3 (extremely well)
   - ☐ 2 (fairly well)
   - ☐ 1 (not well)

4. In the Vocabulary Builder, how well were you able to match the vocabulary words to their synonyms or antonyms?
   - ☐ 3 (extremely well)
   - ☐ 2 (fairly well)
   - ☐ 1 (not well)

5. How well were you able to complete the concept map in the Strategy Follow-up?
   - ☐ 3 (extremely well)
   - ☐ 2 (fairly well)
   - ☐ 1 (not well)

Vocabulary Check

Look back at the work you did in the Vocabulary Builder. Then answer each question by circling the correct letter.

1. *Empty* is a synonym for which of the following words?
   a. collapsed
   b. lashed
   c. hollow

2. Which meaning of the word *buckle* fits this article?
   a. bend or give way
   b. fasten together
   c. clasp that holds things together

3. Which word were you able to figure out by using the context clue "heaps of concrete"?
   a. rots
   b. rubble
   c. drawbacks

4. *Cut apart* is an antonym for which of the following words?
   a. machete
   b. lashed
   c. hollow

5. Which situation describes a drawback of bamboo?
   a. Bamboo burns easily and fast.
   b. Bamboo is stronger than steel.
   c. Bamboo is simple to use.

Add the numbers that you just checked to get your Personal Checklist score. Fill in your score here. Then turn to page 201 and transfer your score onto Graph 1.

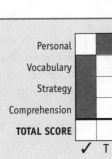

Check your answers with your teacher. Give yourself 1 point for each correct answer, and fill in your Vocabulary score here. Then turn to page 201 and transfer your score onto Graph 1.

Strategy Check

Review the concept map that you created for "Other Problems." Also review the article if necessary. Then answer these questions:

1. Which of the following details did you include on your concept map for "Other Problems"?
   a. bugs
   b. bargain
   c. strong

2. Which detail did you *not* include on your concept map for "Other Problems"?
   a. water
   b. bugs
   c. nonpolluting

3. Which main idea includes the detail that bamboo burns easily and fast?
   a. "Coming into Fashion"
   b. "Some Drawbacks"
   c. "Is Bamboo for You?"

4. If you were to create a concept map for "Is Bamboo for You?" which of these supporting details would you include?
   a. A stalk of bamboo can grow up to three feet per day.
   b. It's hard to understand just how strong bamboo is.
   c. Bamboo homes may never make sense in cold climates.

5. Under which main idea would you find the detail that more builders are interested in using bamboo?
   a. "Coming into Fashion"
   b. "Is Bamboo for You?"
   c. "Super Strong"

Comprehension Check

Review the story if necessary. Then answer these questions:

1. What happened in April 1991, when a big earthquake struck Costa Rica?
   a. All of the homes made of bamboo fell down.
   b. All of the homes made of bamboo remained standing.
   c. All of the homes made of concrete remained standing.

2. Why is bamboo so strong?
   a. because it is tube shaped
   b. because it is very hard
   c. because it is hollow

3. Why do you think builders like working with bamboo?
   a. It burns easily and rots quickly.
   b. It is easy to cut and carry.
   c. It is easy to put together.

4. Which of the following should *not* be made of bamboo?
   a. an apartment building
   b. a home in Costa Rica
   c. a one-story home

5. In which climate is it best to build a bamboo building?
   a. a cold climate
   b. a wet climate
   c. a warm climate

Check your answers with your teacher. Give yourself 1 point for each correct answer, and fill in your Strategy score here. Then turn to page 201 and transfer your score onto Graph 1.

Personal	
Vocabulary	
Strategy	
Comprehension	
TOTAL SCORE	✓ T

Check your answers with your teacher. Give yourself 1 point for each correct answer, and fill in your Comprehension score here. Then turn to page 201 and transfer your score onto Graph 1.

Personal	
Vocabulary	
Strategy	
Comprehension	
TOTAL SCORE	✓ T

Extending

Choose one or both of these activities:

DRAW A PICTURE
Draw a picture of an animal sitting on top of a piece of bamboo. You might draw a picture of an elephant or another large, heavy animal. Then write a funny sentence or two explaining how the animal got there.

RESEARCH COSTA RICA
Choose a partner and research Costa Rica. Use the resources listed on this page or ones that you find yourselves. Look up the answers to these questions:
- Where is Costa Rica located?

- Which countries does it border?

- How many people live there?

- What is the official language?

- What kind of climate does Costa Rica have?

- What kinds of food do Costa Ricans eat?

Share your findings in an oral report. Add any other interesting information that you find. You may want to show maps and pictures of Costa Rica that you have drawn or photocopied.

Resources

Books
Farrelly, David. *The Book of Bamboo.* Sierra Club Books, 1995.

Foley, Erin. *Costa Rica.* Cultures of the World. Benchmark Books, 1997.

LESSON 4 Building Bridges

Building Background

Sometimes in stories, authors use symbols to make a point. A **symbol** is something that stands for something else. For example, a heart is a common symbol for love. In the story you are about to read, the author uses a bridge as a symbol. Of course, you know that a bridge is a structure that is used to cross rivers, lakes, and other bodies of water. Bridges link one area of land to another. As you read "Building Bridges," think about who or what the bridges in the story link.

awesome

boring

grunt

mumbled

partners

propped

sag

scrawny

sturdier

Vocabulary Builder

1. Several of the words in the margin may be familiar to you. Find those words in the statements below. If a statement is true, write **T** on the line beside it. If a statement is false, write **F**.

2. Then, as you read the selection, use context clues to figure out any of the vocabulary words you don't know. Go back and write **T** or **F** next to those sentences. Double-check your earlier work, too, and make any necessary changes.

3. Save your work. You will use it again in the Vocabulary Check.

____ a. A **boring** speech is very interesting.

____ b. **Partners** work with other people.

____ c. A **scrawny** cat can fit inside a small space.

____ d. You could easily hear what I said if I **mumbled** my answer.

____ e. A shirt made of paper is **sturdier** than one made of cloth.

____ f. If a chair is missing a leg, it needs to be **propped** up.

____ g. A **grunt** is a musical sound.

____ h. A couch with broken springs will begin to **sag**.

____ i. If you went to see an **awesome** movie, you would probably fall asleep.

Strategy Builder

Drawing Conclusions About Characters

- A **conclusion** is a decision that you reach after thinking about certain facts or information. When you read a story, you often draw conclusions based on information that the author gives you about the characters, setting, or events.

- You can draw conclusions about the **characters**, or people, in a story by paying attention to what they say, do, think, and feel.

- In many stories, the characters change in some way. As you read the paragraphs below, notice how Kathy changes. See if you can draw any conclusions about her based on what she says and does.

When Kathy's parents asked her to go to the animal shelter to adopt a kitten, she wouldn't go. Ever since she got scratched on the arm, Kathy had hated cats. So her parents left Kathy with her older sister and went to the shelter by themselves.

A while later, Kathy's mom walked into her room with a beautiful gray kitten. Kathy wouldn't look at the kitten, so her mom set it down on the floor. The kitten jumped onto Kathy's lap and began to nuzzle her and purr. Kathy slowly began to pet it. Then she found a little bell and began to play with the kitten. Finally, she said, "I think we should call her Tinkerbell, and I think she should sleep in my room."

Kathy's mother smiled. "Does that mean you don't mind that we adopted a kitten?" she asked.

- If you wanted to track the changes in Kathy's character, you could put them on a **character wheel** like the one below. Notice the conclusions that one reader drew about Kathy. They are in italics.

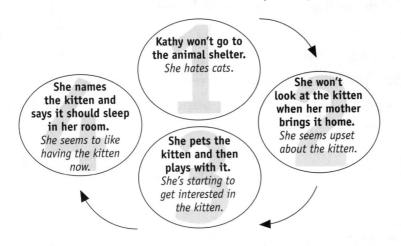

Building Bridges

by Julie Tozier

As you read the first part of this story, notice what the main character says, does, thinks, and feels. What conclusions can you draw about him?

I never gave James Foley much thought. He faded into the walls during class, ate lunch alone in the cafeteria, and hardly ever came to after-school games.

I guess I thought of him the way I thought of Mrs. Kramer's globe. When I came to school, it was always sitting on the bookshelf, but I never felt like bothering with it.

Now I was stuck sitting with James, our desks actually touching, for the whole week. We were building toothpick bridges, and Mrs. Kramer had picked **partners** for us. I thought she'd made a mistake when I saw my name beside James's.

"Hey, Mark!" My best friend Eddie waved from across the room. He pointed to James, laughing like a hyena.

I put my head on my desk. Eddie didn't have to worry. His partner was Ryan Washburn, the smartest kid in fifth grade.

I peeked at James's boots. No laces. He wore them every day. Why couldn't he at least wear sneakers?

"OK, everyone!" Mrs. Kramer yelled cheerfully. Didn't she realize I had nothing to be cheerful about? I lifted my head, but it felt like cement, so I **propped** it in my hands.

"You and your partner will decide who is the architect and who is the transportation person. When the architect has picked out a truss-bridge design, the transportation person can get the glue and toothpicks at the supply table."

I had to be the transportation person because James wouldn't get out of his seat. He looked at the paper Mrs. Kramer passed out. We had about ten bridges to choose from, and James got to pick because he was the architect. He pointed to the plain "warren" design and grunted.

Great, I thought. The most **boring** bridge of all. And to top it off, he was going to grunt at me for a week.

The first day of construction, we built the roadway and piers. James worked pretty fast. He even seemed to know what he was doing.

On the third day, we ran into trouble. We'd used one hundred and twenty toothpicks and two containers of glue, and the sides wouldn't stay up. I was ready to quit.

"Could you get twenty more toothpicks?"

I was so surprised to hear James actually talk that I forgot to answer.

"Hurry up before the whole thing caves in," he said.

I jumped from my seat as if my pants were on fire. As James grunted directions, we made the bottom more stable. This made the sides **sturdier**.

I waited for James to talk again, but he didn't.

On Thursday, the last day of building, Mrs. Kramer announced, "Tomorrow your bridges will be tested for strength by placing a bar across the middle of the bridge, hanging a bucket from the bar, and adding weights slowly to the bucket. As you know, parents and relatives are invited!"

"Who's coming from your family?" I asked James, curious.

I didn't think he was going to answer me. Finally he **mumbled**, "My dad has to work. My mom died."

I sure wished I hadn't asked.

⬣ **Stop here for the Strategy Break.**

Strategy Break

What conclusions can you draw about Mark? How have his feelings changed so far? If you were to begin a character wheel for Mark, it might look like this:

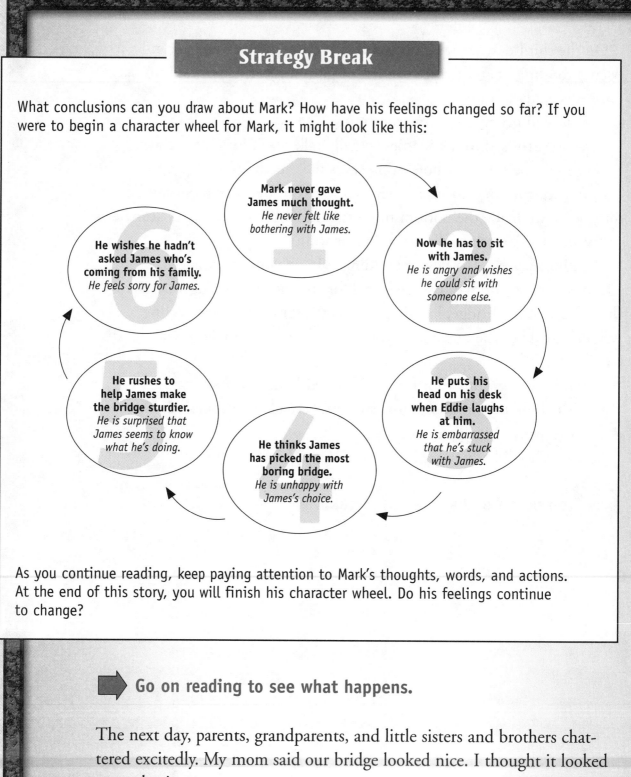

As you continue reading, keep paying attention to Mark's thoughts, words, and actions. At the end of this story, you will finish his character wheel. Do his feelings continue to change?

➡ **Go on reading to see what happens.**

The next day, parents, grandparents, and little sisters and brothers chattered excitedly. My mom said our bridge looked nice. I thought it looked pretty boring.

Mrs. Kramer blew her whistle. The bridge-breaking ceremony had begun!

Two desks were placed side by side a foot apart. Each bridge was placed across the desks so that the bucket hung between them.

Eddie and Ryan were next to last. James and I would be last. Most of the bridges had held three or four pounds.

Everyone cheered when they saw the bridge Eddie and Ryan built. It looked **awesome**. They had used twice as many toothpicks as anyone else.

Their bridge held eight pounds before it buckled. My heart sank to my sneakers.

It was our turn. Eddie poked me in the side as we walked by. "What kind of **scrawny** bridge is that?" he asked, laughing his hyena laugh. He was beginning to bug me.

Then James did something amazing. He stopped, looked at Eddie, and said, "You can't tell something's worth by the way it looks."

Eddie's mouth was hanging open. I watched the back of James's head as he walked up front. I sure hoped he was right.

Mrs. Kramer set up our bridge. It did look pretty scrawny.

I held my breath as she started adding weight. Three pounds. Four. I heard a creak and squeezed my eyes shut—I thought our bridge was breaking. Then I realized it was the classroom door opening.

A man wearing dirty work clothes walked in. He looked a lot like James.

I looked at James. It was the first time I'd ever seen him smile.

Mrs. Kramer had added the fifth pound. Then the sixth.

I stared at James. He glanced proudly at the man standing just inside the door. "My dad builds bridges," he said. "He talks to me about them sometimes."

"How come you never told me before?" I whispered.

"You never asked."

Mrs. Kramer added the seventh pound. Everyone cheered and clapped. The bridge began to **sag**.

"Wait!" I shouted.

Mrs. Kramer stopped, surprised. "But you and James might win!"

"I don't care," I said. "I don't want it to break."

Mrs. Kramer looked at James. "Well?"

James was smiling again, and this time he was smiling at me. "I don't either," he said. ◓

Strategy Follow-up

Work on this activity with a partner or group of classmates. First, on a large piece of paper, draw a character wheel with 10 ovals. Use the information in the Strategy Break to fill in the first 6 ovals. Then use the second part of the story to complete ovals 7–10. Some information is provided below.

Mark's heart sinks when _____ .

He _____

_____ .

He is amazed when _____ _____ .

He _____

_____ .

He shuts his eyes when _____ .

He _____

_____ .

He tells Mrs. Kramer _____ .

He _____

_____ .

✓Personal Checklist

Read each question and put a check (✓) in the correct box.

1. How well do you understand what happened in "Building Bridges"?
   - ☐ 3 (extremely well)
   - ☐ 2 (fairly well)
   - ☐ 1 (not well)

2. After reading Building Background, how well do you understand what the bridge in this story symbolizes?
   - ☐ 3 (extremely well)
   - ☐ 2 (fairly well)
   - ☐ 1 (not well)

3. In the Vocabulary Builder, how many statements did you correctly identify as true or false?
   - ☐ 3 (7–9 statements)
   - ☐ 2 (4–6 statements)
   - ☐ 1 (0–3 statements)

4. How well were you able to complete the character wheel in the Strategy Follow-up?
   - ☐ 3 (extremely well)
   - ☐ 2 (fairly well)
   - ☐ 1 (not well)

5. How well do you understand why Mark did not want the bridge to break?
   - ☐ 3 (extremely well)
   - ☐ 2 (fairly well)
   - ☐ 1 (not well)

Vocabulary Check

Look back at the work you did in the Vocabulary Builder. Then answer each question by circling the correct letter.

1. Mark is unhappy because he thinks that James is going to grunt at him all week. What does *grunt* mean?
   - a. talk without stopping
   - b. talk in a loud voice
   - c. make low, short sounds

2. In the context of this story, which vocabulary word means the opposite of *awesome*?
   - a. scrawny
   - b. boring
   - c. sturdier

3. When Mrs. Kramer adds the seventh pound, the bridge begins to sag. What does *sag* mean?
   - a. rise up
   - b. break
   - c. hang down

4. Who is Mark's partner in this story?
   - a. James
   - b. Eddie
   - c. Mrs. Kramer

5. Which vocabulary word were you able to figure out by using the context clue "I lifted my head, but it felt like cement"?
   - a. propped
   - b. mumbled
   - c. sag

Add the numbers that you just checked to get your Personal Checklist score. Fill in your score here. Then turn to page 201 and transfer your score onto Graph 1.

Check your answers with your teacher. Give yourself 1 point for each correct answer, and fill in your Vocabulary score here. Then turn to page 201 and transfer your score onto Graph 1.

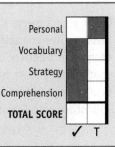

Strategy Check

Review the character wheel that you created for "Building Bridges." Then answer these questions:

1. How does Mark feel about James at the beginning of this story?

   a. He never felt like bothering with James.

   b. He wants to get to know James better.

   c. He respects and looks up to James.

2. Which of Mark's thoughts could have led you to believe he was beginning to change his mind about James?

   a. Mark wonders why James couldn't at least wear sneakers.

   b. Mark thinks James has picked the most boring bridge of all.

   c. Mark wishes he hadn't asked about James's family.

3. Which sentence describes why Mark is amazed?

   a. James talks to Eddie.

   b. James wears sneakers to school.

   c. James laughs at their bridge.

4. How does Mark feel about James by the end of the story?

   a. By the end of the story, Mark hates James.

   b. By the end of the story, Mark likes James.

   c. By the end of the story, Mark feels sorry for James.

5. Which group of words describes Mark's changing feelings toward James in this story?

   a. disinterest, dislike, hatred

   b. disinterest, understanding, caring

   c. disinterest, dislike, disinterest

Comprehension Check

Review the story if necessary. Then answer these questions:

1. At the beginning of the story, why is Mark unhappy?

   a. He has to wear boots with no laces.

   b. He has to sit next to Eddie.

   c. He has to build a bridge with James.

2. Why does Mark wish he hadn't asked about James's family?

   a. because Mark didn't want to know about James's family

   b. because the question probably made James feel sad

   c. because James wouldn't answer the question

3. How does James feel when his father comes into the classroom?

   a. proud and happy

   b. embarrassed and sad

   c. bored and angry

4. Why doesn't Mark want the bridge to break?

   a. because he doesn't want to lose to Eddie and Ryan

   b. because he and James built the bridge together

   c. because the bridge was so hard to build

5. What do you think James and Mark's bridge symbolizes at the end of the story?

   a. the arrival of James's father

   b. the dislike that Mark feels for James

   c. the relationship Mark and James have built

Check your answers with your teacher. Give yourself 1 point for each correct answer, and fill in your Strategy score here. Then turn to page 201 and transfer your score onto Graph 1.

Personal	
Vocabulary	
Strategy	
Comprehension	
TOTAL SCORE	

✓ T

Check your answers with your teacher. Give yourself 1 point for each correct answer, and fill in your Comprehension score here. Then turn to page 201 and transfer your score onto Graph 1.

Personal	
Vocabulary	
Strategy	
Comprehension	
TOTAL SCORE	

✓ T

Extending

Choose one or both of these activities:

BUILD A TOOTHPICK BRIDGE

Get together with a partner and build a bridge out of toothpicks. Do some research on bridges first, and choose the design you want to build. (See the book listed on this page for ideas.) Then gather a supply of toothpicks and glue. Build the bridge on a piece of heavy cardboard. When your bridge is finished, display it in your classroom. If you'd like, you can test its strength the way the students did in the story. How many pounds does your bridge hold?

WRITE A SEQUEL

What do you think happened the day after the bridge-breaking ceremony? What, if anything, did Mark and James say to each other? How did they act? Write the sequel to this story. Tell what happens to Mark and James. Use the resources listed on this page if you need help getting started.

Resources

Books

Dupre, Judith. *Bridges*. Black Dog & Leventhal, 1997.

Pollard, Jeanne. *Building Toothpick Bridges*. Math Project Series. Dale Seymour Publications, 1985.

Web Sites

http://science.howstuffworks.com/bridge.html
This site provides an in-depth look at how beam and suspension bridges work.

http://www.brantacan.co.uk
Click on "Bridges." Here you can find photographs, diagrams, and explanations of the basic types of bridges. You can download computer programs about bridge models and bridge behavior. There are also links to other Web sites about bridges, including some sites about building model bridges.

http://www.pbs.org/wgbh/nova/bridge/build.html
Learn about the four steps to building a bridge. Play architect and engineer with an online game.

LESSON ⑤ Bridges

Building Background

What do you know about bridges? Probably more than you think. Picture the bridges in your community or state. Think about famous bridges all over the world. What are their names? What are they made of? What do they look like?

Fill in the first column of the chart with at least three things you know about bridges. Then fill in the second column with three questions that you hope the selection will answer about bridges. After you finish reading, you will fill in the last column with what you learned.

Bridges

K (What I **K**now)	W (What I **W**ant to Know)	L (What I **L**earned)
1.	1.	1.
2.	2.	2.
3.	3.	3.

anchorages

arch

beam bridges

cables

clapper bridges

deck

hanging bridges

piers

suspension

bridges

towers

Vocabulary Builder

1. When you read nonfiction, you often come across words that are related to the topic of the selection. Those words are called **specialized vocabulary**.

2. Sometimes you can use context clues to figure out the specialized vocabulary. At other times, you can picture what's being described. For example, read this paragraph from "Bridges." What do you picture as you read?

Our first real bridges were probably trees, which had fallen across streams. These natural bridges may well have given us the idea of making simple wooden **beam bridges.** Then, when a stream was too wide to be spanned by a single log or plank, these early bridge builders used two or more beams to reach the other side. These planks were supported by wooden logs, called **piers,** standing upright in the water.

3. On another sheet of paper, draw a picture of what you just read. Label your picture with the **boldfaced** words in the paragraph.

4. Then, as you read "Bridges," use context clues and your own drawings to help you understand the other boldfaced words. If context and drawings don't help, try to find a diagram of a bridge in a book or an encyclopedia.

5. Save your work. You will use it again in the Vocabulary Check.

Strategy Builder

Comparing and Contrasting While You Read

- Authors often compare and contrast things when they write. **Comparing** means looking at how two or more things are similar, or alike. **Contrasting** means looking at how two or more things are different.

- Making a **comparison chart** while you read can help you keep track of how things are alike and different. For example, if you were reading an article about baseball, hockey, and basketball, your chart might look like this:

	Equipment	Playing Areas	Scoring
Baseball	baseball bat baseball glove	outdoors—grass or artificial turf	1 run = 1 point
Hockey	hockey stick puck	indoors or outdoors—ice	1 goal = 1 point
Basketball	basketball	indoors or outdoors— hard surface	1 basket = 2 points

- The chart helps you easily compare and contrast the equipment, playing areas, and scoring used in each sport. For example, you can see that both hockey and basketball can be played indoors or outdoors. You also can see that baseball and basketball are played with a kind of ball, while hockey is played with a puck.

Bridges

by Graham Rickard

As you read this selection, apply what you have learned about comparing and contrasting. The first section tells about the first bridges ever built. As you read, notice the types, materials, and uses for those early bridges.

The First Bridges

Crossing natural obstacles, such as rivers and deep valleys, has always been a challenge to people. Our first real bridges were probably trees, which had fallen across streams. These natural bridges may well have given us the idea of making simple wooden **beam bridges**. Then, when a stream was too wide to be spanned by a single log or plank, these early bridge builders used two or more beams to reach the other side. These planks were supported by wooden logs, called **piers**, standing upright in the water.

In areas where trees were scarce, similar bridges were built from large slabs of stone. The world's oldest surviving bridges of this kind can still be seen on Dartmoor in England. They are called clam or **clapper bridges**.

In China, India and South America, people developed the art of building **hanging bridges** from ropes and creepers. These materials do not last very long, but these early bridges were the forerunners of our modern **suspension bridges**.

Throughout the ages, new transportation systems developed, such as railroads, canals and main roads. Each new system needed a whole new generation of bridges, using new techniques, styles and materials to build them even longer and stronger than before.

⬢ **Stop here for the Strategy Break.**

Strategy Break

If you were to begin a comparison chart for the bridges you've read about so far, it might look like this:

Bridges

	Materials	Uses
Beam	wood	crossing natural obstacles
Clam or Clapper	stone	crossing natural obstacles
Hanging	ropes and creepers	crossing natural obstacles

As you read the next two sections of "Bridges," keep track of the types, materials, and uses of Roman and modern bridges. At the end of this selection, you will use that information in a comparison chart of your own.

 Go on reading.

Roman Bridges

Besides being great fighters, the soldiers of the Roman Army were great engineers. They became very skilled at bridge-building, and when Julius Caesar invaded Gaul, his army built a bridge across the Rhine River in only ten days.

When the Romans invaded parts of Asia, they discovered the secret of building a stone **arch**. The arch is a very strong shape and its strength led to a great change in bridge-building techniques. It enabled the Romans to build much longer bridges, with fewer piers between each span. Because these new arched bridges were built of stone or brick, they lasted much longer than the older wooden bridges, and many fine examples can still be seen today. In Rome itself, six fine stone bridges remain out of the eight that the Romans built over the Tiber River.

One of the things that helped these bridges to last so long was the Romans' discovery of cement concrete. They used a mixture of volcanic soil, lime and water, which would set hard even under water and enabled their engineers to build very strong piers for their bridges. In the nineteenth century it was discovered that concrete could be made strong enough to build entire bridges by reinforcing it with iron bars. Today reinforced concrete is one of the main materials used to build bridges.

Modern Bridges

The great increase in road traffic during the twentieth century has forced almost every country to modernize and improve its road systems, creating thousands of miles of highways. This has involved the building of many new types of road bridges, using the very latest materials.

The world's longest spans are all suspension bridges, which rely totally on the strength of steel. They vary in design, but all suspension bridges, from the most primitive rope crossings to the very latest steel structures, have three basic elements—**cables**, **towers** and **anchorages**. The cables support the weight of the **deck** and the traffic that passes over the bridge. The towers, made of wood, stone, or steel, hold up the cables, which pass over the top of them. The anchorages fasten the cables to the ground, and their weight and strength are very important to the safety of the bridge.

Suspension bridges sway in the wind. This caused a disaster in the United States in 1940, when the new Tacoma Narrows Bridge started to twist in a gale. It finally broke up, ripping loose from its cables and crashing into the waters below. But the knowledge gained from this disaster led to new safer designs for future bridges. Today, the longest suspension bridge is the Humber Estuary Bridge in England. It spans 1,410 m (4,626 ft). In the future, longer bridges will certainly be built.

Not all modern bridges are of the suspension type. They can be of arch, beam, or cantilever designs, depending on the length of the span and the purpose of the bridge. Reinforced concrete is often used on major highways to make beam bridges and overpasses, and Waterloo Bridge in London is an example of a graceful concrete arch. The largest concrete arch of all spans 304.8 m (1,000 ft) of water. This is the Gladesville Bridge in Sydney, Australia. Nearby is the famous arch of the Sydney Harbour Bridge, which is made of steel. The deck of this bridge hangs by thick steel rods from a massive steel arch. The Thousand Island Bridge, linking Canada and the United States across the St. Lawrence River, is a mixture of three types of bridges. It uses suspension, a steel arch and strengthened beams.

New materials will probably be used in the near future to make bridges longer, stronger and lighter than was ever thought possible in the past. Massive bridges linking, for example, Italy with the island of Sicily will become possible for the first time. What is certain is that bridges will continue to evolve, and that engineers will make the best of new materials and techniques. ●

Strategy Follow-up

First, go back to page 46 and fill in the last column of the K-W-L chart. List at least three things that you learned about bridges.

Next, complete the comparison chart below. When you finish the chart, look it over. In what ways are all the bridges the same? In what ways are they different?

Bridges

	Materials	Uses
Early Beam	wood	crossing natural obstacles
Clam or Clapper	stone	crossing natural obstacles
Hanging	ropes and creepers	crossing natural obstacles
Roman Arch		
Modern Suspension		
Modern Beam		
Modern Arch		

✓Personal Checklist

Read each question and put a check (✓) in the correct box.

1. How well do you understand the information in "Bridges"?
   - ☐ 3   (extremely well)
   - ☐ 2   (fairly well)
   - ☐ 1   (not well)

2. On the K-W-L chart, how easily were you able to list at least three things that you learned from this selection?
   - ☐ 3   (extremely well)
   - ☐ 2   (fairly well)
   - ☐ 1   (not well)

3. By the time you finished reading this selection, how many specialized vocabulary words were you able to figure out?
   - ☐ 3   (9–11 words)
   - ☐ 2   (5–8 words)
   - ☐ 1   (0–4 words)

4. How well were you able to complete the comparison chart in the Strategy Follow-up?
   - ☐ 3   (extremely well)
   - ☐ 2   (fairly well)
   - ☐ 1   (not well)

5. How well do you understand how bridges have developed over time?
   - ☐ 3   (extremely well)
   - ☐ 2   (fairly well)
   - ☐ 1   (not well)

Vocabulary Check

Look back at the work you did in the Vocabulary Builder. Then answer each question by circling the correct letter.

1. Which specialized vocabulary word describes a type of bridge that sways in the wind?
   a. suspension bridge
   b. clapper bridge
   c. beam bridge

2. Which word describes the parts of a beam bridge that stand upright in the water?
   a. cables
   b. anchorages
   c. piers

3. Which of the following enabled the Romans to build much longer bridges?
   a. towers
   b. arches
   c. cables

4. In the context of this selection, what does the word *deck* mean?
   a. pack of cards
   b. tape player
   c. floor

5. In suspension bridges, which structures hold up the cables?
   a. piers
   b. anchorages
   c. towers

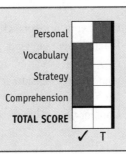

Add the numbers that you just checked to get your Personal Checklist score. Fill in your score here. Then turn to page 201 and transfer your score onto Graph 1.

Check your answers with your teacher. Give yourself 1 point for each correct answer, and fill in your Vocabulary score here. Then turn to page 201 and transfer your score onto Graph 1.

Strategy Check

Review the comparison chart you completed for "Bridges." Then answer these questions:

1. According to your comparison chart, which was the first bridge to be built with concrete?

    a. early beam

    b. Roman arch

    c. modern suspension

2. Which bridge, made of ropes and creepers (vines), was a kind of suspension bridge?

    a. early beam

    b. hanging

    c. clam or clapper

3. Compare the uses of bridges throughout history. What use is common to *every* bridge?

    a. invading countries during war

    b. improving road traffic

    c. crossing natural obstacles

4. What are many modern bridges made of?

    a. steel

    b. wood

    c. stone

5. What material discovered by the Romans is still used in bridges today?

    a. ropes

    b. steel

    c. concrete

Comprehension Check

Review the selection if necessary. Then answer these questions:

1. Which of these building materials lasts the least amount of time?

    a. steel

    b. wood

    c. rope

2. What did Roman engineers use to strengthen the piers under their bridges?

    a. reinforced concrete

    b. volcanic soil, lime, and water

    c. iron bars

3. How did the collapse of the Tacoma Narrows Bridge improve future bridges?

    a. The disaster led to safer designs.

    b. The disaster put an end to suspension bridges.

    c. The disaster led to the discovery of concrete.

4. Which bridge has the largest concrete arch in the world?

    a. the Waterloo Bridge in London, England

    b. the Gladesville Bridge in Sydney, Australia

    c. the Sydney Harbour Bridge in Sydney, Australia

5. How have new materials improved bridges?

    a. They've made them longer, stronger, and lighter.

    b. They've made them much harder to build.

    c. They've made them much more dangerous.

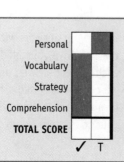

Check your answers with your teacher. Give yourself 1 point for each correct answer, and fill in your Strategy score here. Then turn to page 201 and transfer your score onto Graph 1.

Personal
Vocabulary
Strategy
Comprehension
TOTAL SCORE
✓ T

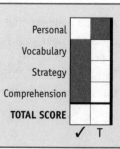

Check your answers with your teacher. Give yourself 1 point for each correct answer, and fill in your Comprehension score here. Then turn to page 201 and transfer your score onto Graph 1.

Personal
Vocabulary
Strategy
Comprehension
TOTAL SCORE
✓ T

Extending

Choose one or more of these activities:

WRITE A BOOK

Using the resources on this page or ones you find yourself, gather information about a particular bridge. Find out what type of bridge it is and when it was built. Find out what materials were used to build the bridge and what it is used for. Draw a picture of the bridge, or find photos or diagrams of it. Bind all your information into a book, and share it with the class.

DRAW A MAP OF ANCIENT ROME

Julius Caesar helped make Rome the center of a large empire. The Roman Empire reached its greatest power from A.D. 96 to A.D. 180. Find out what territories the Romans controlled around that time. Then draw a map showing the Roman Empire at the height of its power. If you can, include the bridges that existed in that area.

BUILD A BRIDGE

Build an arched bridge out of clay. Use clay piers between the arches to hold up the bridge. Try to make the bridge about a foot long. Use the resources listed on this page if you need help getting started.

Resources

Books

Chrisp, Peter. *The Roman Empire.* Make It Work! History Series. Two-Can Publishing, 2001.

Ricciuti, Edward R. *America's Top 10 Bridges.* America's Top 10. Blackbirch Marketing, 1998.

Web Sites

http://www.nireland.com/bridgeman
This site has photos and information about bridge history, design, and materials. It includes a dictionary of terms.

http://www.roman-empire.net/children
This site includes sections on Roman history, achievements, architecture, and maps. There also are links to picture tours and class projects.

Learning New Words

VOCABULARY

From Lesson 1
- notepaper
- sunbeams
- sundial
- tiptoe

From Lesson 3
- drawbacks

From Lesson 4
- awesome/
  boring

Compound Words

A compound word is made of two words put together. In "The Mystery in the Attic," Greg and Molly find a message written on a piece of notepaper. *Notepaper* is made from the words *note* and *paper* and means "paper used for writing notes or messages."

Fill in each blank with a compound word by combining a word from Row 1 with a word from Row 2.

Row 1:   rain   dew   boy   dinner   base
Row 2:   friend   coat   drops   ball   time

1. game played on a "diamond" = _____

2. clothing worn during a storm = _____

3. tiny beads of moisture = _____

4. when the main meal is eaten = _____

5. male companion = _____

Antonyms

An antonym is a word that means the opposite of another word. In "Building Bridges," Mark uses the words *awesome* and *boring* to describe opposite kinds of bridges. Mark thinks Eddie and Ryan's bridge is awesome, but he thinks his and James's bridge is boring.

Draw a line from each word in Column 1 to its antonym in Column 2.

COLUMN 1	COLUMN 2
question	finish
huge	strong
sunny	cloudy
peaceful	tiny
weak	answer
start	noisy

Multiple-Meaning Words

VOCABULARY

From Lesson 2
- blade
- handle
- rings

From Lesson 3
- buckle
- lashed

From Lesson 4
- deck
- piers
- towers

A single word can have more than one meaning. For example, the word *bridge* can mean "a card game" or "a part of the nose" or "a structure built across water." To figure out which meaning of *bridge* an author is using, you have to use context. Context is the information surrounding a word or situation that helps you understand its meaning.

When you read "Building Bridges," you used context to figure out that the author uses *bridge* to mean two different things. She means "a structure built across water," but she also uses *bridge* as a symbol to describe the relationship that Mark and James build as they work on their structure.

Use context to figure out the correct meaning of each underlined word. Circle the letter of the correct meaning.

1. Sheila tried to make a whistle out of a <u>blade</u> of grass.

   a. flat, wide leaf

   b. the cutting part of a tool or weapon

2. Jack <u>lashed</u> his horse when it wouldn't run any faster.

   a. tied with a rope or cord

   b. hit with a whip

3. I couldn't <u>buckle</u> my shoe because the piece of metal was broken.

   a. bend or bulge

   b. fasten together

4. We formed a <u>ring</u> around the couple as we sang them a song.

   a. circle of people

   b. piece of jewelry

Just a Girl

floundered

minaret

mosque

mountainside

prayer

scooped up

squinted

terraced fields

Yemeni village

CLIPBOARD

The Setting

CLIPBOARD

Islamic Religion

CLIPBOARD

Halima's Actions

Building Background

The selection you are about to read takes place in Yemen. Yemen is a country that lies to the south of Saudi Arabia. The people of Yemen speak Arabic. Most Yemenis are Muslims. That means they follow the Islamic religion. In small Yemeni villages, girls and boys are often treated differently. Boys go to school and learn to read and write. Girls stay home and learn to be good housekeepers and mothers.

In "Just a Girl," the main character—Halima—wants to learn how to do more. She wants to prove she can do things that her brothers can do.

When have you been told that you couldn't do something because you were "just a child"? Get together with a partner and talk about your experiences. What weren't you allowed to do? How did that make you feel? How did you prove that you weren't "just a child"?

Vocabulary Builder

1. Before you begin reading "Just a Girl," read the vocabulary words in the margin. Write any of the words that you already know on the appropriate clipboards.

2. Then, as you read the story, find the rest of the vocabulary words. Read them in context and decide what they mean. If using context doesn't help, look up the words in a dictionary. Then write them on the appropriate clipboards.

3. Save your work. You will use it again in the Vocabulary Check.

Strategy Builder

Identifying Problems and Solutions in Stories

- In some stories, the main character or characters have a **problem**. Throughout the story, the characters try to solve the problem. Sometimes they must try more than one **solution**. By the end of the story, they usually come up with the solution that works—the **end result**.

- As you read the following paragraph, notice Mark's problem and how he tries to solve it.

> Mark had to write a report on Yemen, but he didn't know anything about it. He asked his mother to drive him to the library, but she told him that her car was in the shop for repairs. He decided to ride his bike to the library, but he discovered that it had a flat tire. Suddenly Mark had an idea. He turned on his computer and searched the Internet. He found lots of information on Yemen. He printed out what he needed and started writing his report.

- If you wanted to highlight the problem and solutions in the paragraph above, you could put them on a **problem-solution frame**. It would look like this:

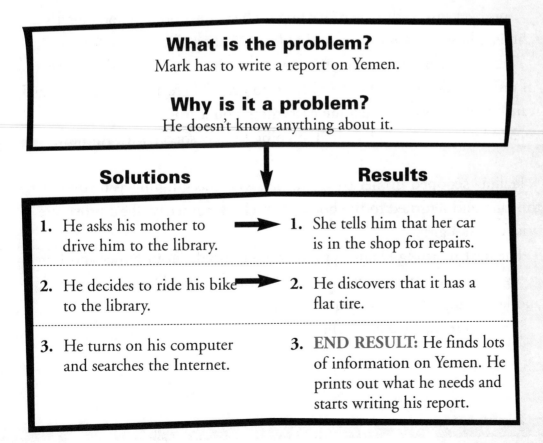

What is the problem?
Mark has to write a report on Yemen.

Why is it a problem?
He doesn't know anything about it.

Solutions	Results
1. He asks his mother to drive him to the library.	**1.** She tells him that her car is in the shop for repairs.
2. He decides to ride his bike to the library.	**2.** He discovers that it has a flat tire.
3. He turns on his computer and searches the Internet.	**3.** END RESULT: He finds lots of information on Yemen. He prints out what he needs and starts writing his report.

Just a Girl

by Brenda S. Cox

As you read the first part of "Just a Girl," apply the strategies that you just learned. Try to identify the problem Halima faces. Think about the impact that the story's setting has on her problem.

Halima and her younger brother Ahmad scratched in the dirt with sticks. The tall houses of their **Yemeni village** blended into the **mountainside**. White-rimmed windows stared past the children down a giant staircase of **terraced fields**.

Ahmad wrote carefully in the sand: "Baa, Alif, Baa: bab." Nine-year-old Halima tried to copy the Arabic word for "door." When Ahmad laughed at her squiggly letters, she traced them again.

"There!" she shouted. "I wrote it."

"Well," said Ahmad, "it's not bad for a girl."

"I could write as well as you if Father would let me go to school," retorted Halima. She hiked up the embroidered pants under her purple dress.

"School! But you're just a girl. No girls from our village have ever gone to school. You have to stay home to help Mother. Anyway, a girl would get tired walking so far."

"I could do it."

"You'd get lost in the town. It's huge! There are a boys' school, a girls' school, a hospital, a **mosque**, and at least 20 shops."

Halima sighed. She twisted the material of her dress around her finger. "If only I could go to school and learn to read. There are so many things I want to know. Will you tell me everything you learn?"

"Maybe later," Ahmad said. "I'm going to play soccer with Ali now. Bye!"

Halima **scooped up** her baby brother, who was gurgling as he dug in the sand and returned to the house. Somehow, someday, she'd prove she wasn't "just a girl!"

The next morning Halima's mother announced, "Your father and I are going to my parents' village today with your cousins. Do the housework, and keep baby Yahya out of trouble."

"I'll be careful, Mama," Halima promised.

When everyone had gone, Halima did her morning chores. She swept the floors clean and arranged the mafraj cushions. She fed the cow, sheep, and chickens. She gathered eggs and brought in firewood.

After baking bread for lunch, Halima went down the hill to fetch water. She balanced the water jar on her head, picked up Yahya, and made her way up to the house without spilling a drop.

At the front door, she sat down to rest. Thankful for his freedom, Yahya crawled off to explore the rocks nearby. Suddenly he began screaming. Halima caught her breath. A big brown scorpion was on Yahya's arm. Swallowing her fear, Halima brushed off the ugly creature and smashed it with a rock.

She picked up the baby and tried to comfort him, but it was no use. He screamed louder with pain. She could see the tiny stinger in his arm. Halima tried to pull it out, but the stinger only went in deeper.

What could she do? Last year a baby in her village had died of a scorpion sting!

All her relatives had left in the village's only car. Her brothers were at school. She would have to take the baby to the doctor herself. How would her parents know where she had gone?

⬣ **Stop here for the Strategy Break.**

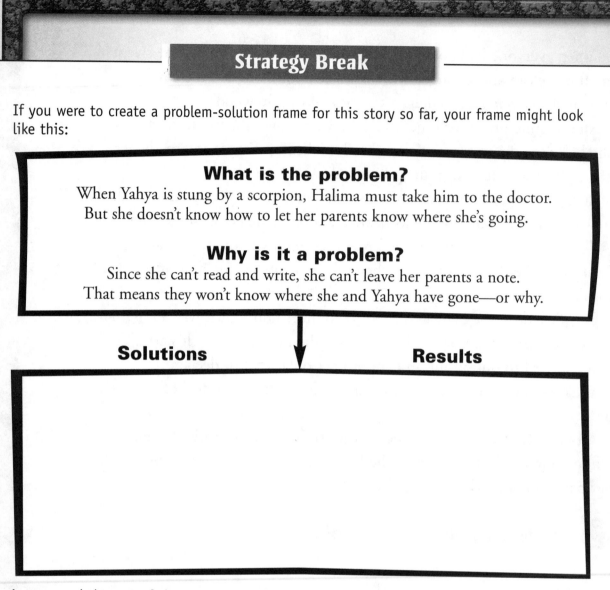

Strategy Break

If you were to create a problem-solution frame for this story so far, your frame might look like this:

What is the problem?
When Yahya is stung by a scorpion, Halima must take him to the doctor.
But she doesn't know how to let her parents know where she's going.

Why is it a problem?
Since she can't read and write, she can't leave her parents a note.
That means they won't know where she and Yahya have gone—or why.

Solutions   **Results**

As you read the rest of the story, pay attention to how Halima solves her problem. Keep track of her solutions, the results of those solutions, and the end result. When you finish the story, you will use the information to complete a problem-solution frame of your own.

➡ **Go on reading to see what happens.**

Halima picked up the stick she used for "lessons" with Ahmad. In the dirt she drew pictures of a baby and a scorpion with its tail pointing toward the baby. How could she show the town? The closest mosque was in town; that would be easy to draw. In Ahmad's book she had seen one with a tower called a **minaret** for calling people to **prayer**. She drew a minaret, hoping her parents would understand this message.

The doctor might need to see the scorpion. Shuddering, she wrapped the dead scorpion in a cloth and tied it to the sash of her dress.

She carried her crying brother back down the steep path. As she passed the water tank, she **floundered** over stones. Thorns caught at her pants and scratched her sandaled feet. Finally, she reached the paved road to town. She raced along it until she was almost exhausted. Yahya, whimpering now, felt heavier and heavier.

She hurried on and on until she noticed a white building. Halima **squinted** at the sign. Surely it was a word her brother had taught her. Yes, it was "mustashfa," "hospital!" Thankfully, Halima stumbled through the door.

Late that evening, Halima's father found his daughter nearly asleep by Yahya's hospital bed.

"She's a brave girl and intelligent too," Halima heard the doctor whisper to her father. "She even brought the scorpion so we knew exactly how to treat the baby. It was a serious sting. The little boy might have died if she hadn't brought him here so quickly."

Her father watched Halima and his son for a while. At last he said, "I saw your message and came right away. Halima, I'm proud of you. You'll be a good mother someday."

"I knew how to find the hospital because Ahmad taught me to read the word."

"Is that right? Well, maybe a little learning wouldn't hurt you, even if you are just a girl. Do you still want to go to that school?"

"Oh, Father!" Halima said, flinging her arms around him.

Soon Halima was the happiest, hardest-working girl in first grade. ●

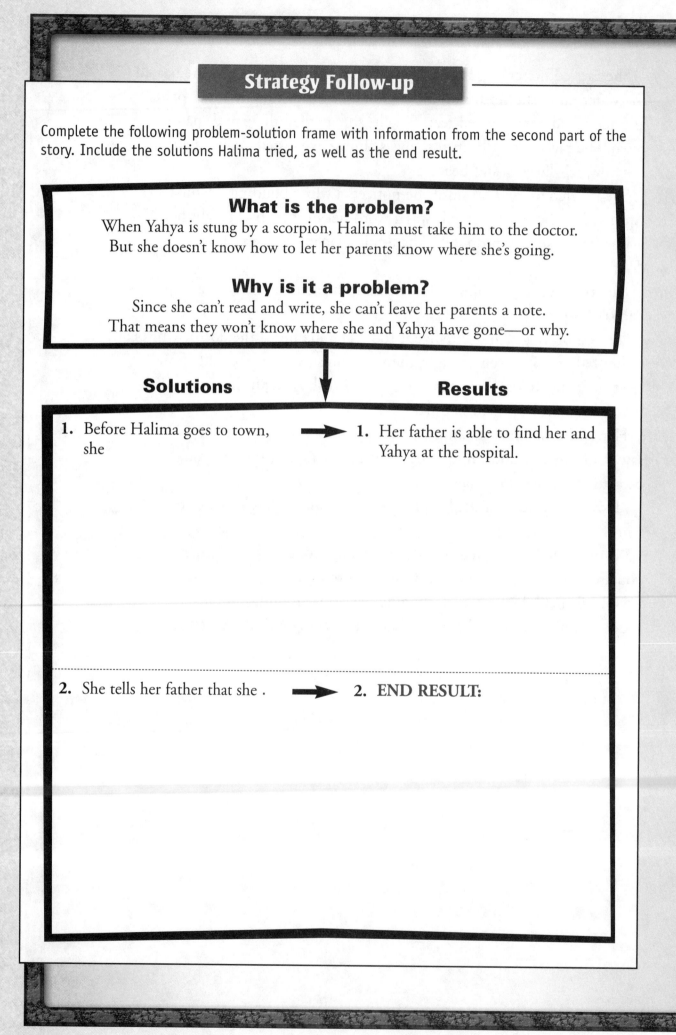

Strategy Follow-up

Complete the following problem-solution frame with information from the second part of the story. Include the solutions Halima tried, as well as the end result.

What is the problem?
When Yahya is stung by a scorpion, Halima must take him to the doctor.
But she doesn't know how to let her parents know where she's going.

Why is it a problem?
Since she can't read and write, she can't leave her parents a note.
That means they won't know where she and Yahya have gone—or why.

Solutions   **Results**

1. Before Halima goes to town, she

   1. Her father is able to find her and Yahya at the hospital.

2. She tells her father that she .

   2. **END RESULT:**

✓Personal Checklist

Read each question and put a check (✓) in the correct box.

1. How well do you understand what happened in "Just a Girl"?
   - ☐ 3 (extremely well)
   - ☐ 2 (fairly well)
   - ☐ 1 (not well)

2. How well did the information in Building Background help you understand why Halima can't read or write?
   - ☐ 3 (extremely well)
   - ☐ 2 (fairly well)
   - ☐ 1 (not well)

3. By the time you finished reading this story, how many vocabulary words were you able to write on the appropriate clipboards?
   - ☐ 3 (7–9 words)
   - ☐ 2 (4–6 words)
   - ☐ 1 (0–3 words)

4. How well were you able to complete the problem-solution frame in the Strategy Follow-up?
   - ☐ 3 (extremely well)
   - ☐ 2 (fairly well)
   - ☐ 1 (not well)

5. How well do you understand why Halima's father changes his mind about his daughter's schooling at the end of the story?
   - ☐ 3 (extremely well)
   - ☐ 2 (fairly well)
   - ☐ 1 (not well)

Vocabulary Check

Look back at the work you did in the Vocabulary Builder. Then answer each question by circling the correct letter.

1. Which vocabulary word is a related to the Islamic religion?
   - a. Yemeni village
   - b. terraced fields
   - c. mosque

2. As Halima carried her crying brother, she floundered over the stones on the path. What does *floundered* mean?
   - a. struggled awkwardly
   - b. ran quickly
   - c. looked carefully

3. Which vocabulary word were you able to figure out by using the context clue "tower"?
   - a. prayer
   - b. minaret
   - c. mountainside

4. On which clipboard did you write the words *mountainside, terraced fields,* and *Yemeni village*?
   - a. Words that Describe the Setting
   - b. Words Related to the Islamic Religion
   - c. Words that Describe Halima's Actions

5. When Halima came to a white building, she squinted at the sign on it. What does it mean to *squint*?
   - a. open the eyes wide
   - b. wrinkle the nose
   - c. scrunch up the eyes

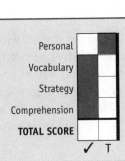

Add the numbers that you just checked to get your Personal Checklist score. Fill in your score here. Then turn to page 201 and transfer your score onto Graph 1.

Personal
Vocabulary
Strategy
Comprehension
TOTAL SCORE
✓ T

Check your answers with your teacher. Give yourself 1 point for each correct answer, and fill in your Vocabulary score here. Then turn to page 201 and transfer your score onto Graph 1.

Personal
Vocabulary
Strategy
Comprehension
TOTAL SCORE
✓ T

Strategy Check

Review the problem-solution frame that you completed in the Strategy Follow-up. Then answer these questions:

1. When Yahya gets stung by the scorpion, why is it a problem that Halima cannot read and write?

    a. She doesn't know how to write, so she can't leave her parents a note.

    b. She doesn't know how read, so she can't read all the signs on the buildings.

    c. Both of the above answers are correct.

2. What is the first solution that Halima tries in order to solve her problem?

    a. She finds the hospital.

    b. She draws pictures in the dirt.

    c. She goes to school.

3. What is the result of Halima's message in the dirt?

    a. Her brother gets stung by a scorpion.

    b. She wraps the dead scorpion in a cloth.

    c. Her father is able to find her and Yahya.

4. What is the end result of Halima's problem?

    a. Her father lets her go to school to learn to read and write.

    b. She doesn't want to go to school anymore.

    c. She gets scolded for taking Yahya to the hospital.

5. If Halima hadn't told her father how she was able to find the hospital, how might the end result have been different?

    a. She might never want to go to school.

    b. Her father might never have scolded her.

    c. Her father might never have sent her to school.

Comprehension Check

Review the story if necessary. Then answer these questions:

1. Why doesn't Halima write as well as her brother Ahmad?

    a. because she doesn't want to learn

    b. because she doesn't go to school

    c. because she'd rather do housework

2. Why doesn't Ahmad think his sister should go to school?

    a. because no girls from their village had ever gone to school

    b. because he wants to teach her himself

    c. because there is only a school in town for boys

3. What does Halima do when she sees a scorpion on Yahya's arm?

    a. She sits down to rest and lets Yahya cry.

    b. She brushes the scorpion off and smashes it.

    c. She draws a picture of the scorpion in the dirt.

4. Why does Halima draw a minaret in the dirt?

    a. She is trying to tell her parents to pray for Yahya.

    b. She is trying to tell her parents she's taking Yahya to a mosque.

    c. She is trying to tell her parents she's taking Yahya into town.

5. Which words best describe Halima?

    a. slow and frightened

    b. selfish and uncaring

    c. quick-thinking and brave

Check your answers with your teacher. Give yourself 1 point for each correct answer, and fill in your Strategy score here. Then turn to page 201 and transfer your score onto Graph 1.

Personal		
Vocabulary		
Strategy		
Comprehension		
TOTAL SCORE	✓	T

Check your answers with your teacher. Give yourself 1 point for each correct answer, and fill in your Comprehension score here. Then turn to page 201 and transfer your score onto Graph 1.

Personal		
Vocabulary		
Strategy		
Comprehension		
TOTAL SCORE	✓	T

Extending

Choose one or both of these activities:

REPORT ON YEMEN

Prepare a report on Yemen that you can present to the class. Use some of the resources listed on this page if you'd like. Answer these questions in your report:

- On which continent is Yemen located?

- Which countries and bodies of water surround Yemen?

- What is the name of its capital?

- How do people enter and leave the capital?

- How many people live in Yemen?

- How do most Yemeni people make a living?

Find Yemen on a map or globe, and point it out to the class.

MAKE A BROCHURE

Would you know what to do if you were stung by a scorpion? Do some research and find out. Then make a brochure that gives information about scorpions and how to treat their stings.

Resources

Book

Yemen . . . in Pictures. Visual Geography Series. Lerner Publications, 1993.

Web Sites

http://www.members.aol.com/yalnet/pictures.html
This site is a gallery of photos of Yemen and the Yemeni people.

http://www.yemenembassy.org.uk
This site of the Yemen Embassy in the United Kingdom has facts about the land, people, and culture of Yemen.

L. Frank Baum (Part 1)

Building Background

You've probably seen the movie *The Wizard of Oz*. It tells the story of Dorothy and her companions and their adventures in the Land of Oz. The movie is based on a book by L. Frank Baum. Baum wrote about witches and other scary things in his books. But when he was a child, thinking and reading about scary things gave him bad dreams.

What were you frightened of when you were very small? Did you think that some creature lived in your closet or under your bed? Did it only come out at night when you were alone? Did you dream about it? In the margin, draw a picture of what the creature might have looked like. Or draw a picture of some other scary creature that you've seen in a book or movie.

fairy tales

goblins

make-believe

nightmare

scarecrow

spooky

witch

Vocabulary Builder

1. The words in the margin are all from the selection that you are about to read. Many of the words are often found in scary stories. On a separate sheet of paper, write your own scary story using as many of the words as you can. If you'd like, you can write about the creature that you drew for Building Background.

2. When you have finished reading this selection, read your own story again. How many vocabulary words did you use? Did you use them correctly? If necessary, rewrite parts of your story. Fix any parts that contain words used incorrectly, or add parts to include any words you didn't know.

3. Save your story. You will use it again in the Vocabulary Check.

Strategy Builder

How to Read a Biography

- In this lesson and Lesson 8, you will read a biography of L. Frank Baum. A **biography** tells the story of a real person's life, and is written by someone else.

- The events in most biographies are told in the **sequence**, or time order, in which they happened. To make that sequence as clear as possible, authors often use **signal words**. Some signal words—such as *then, next,* and *a short time later*—help you link one smaller event to the next in a biography. However, signal words such as *When he was twelve* or *in 1886* help you see the sequence of the major, or most important, events in a person's life.

- The following paragraphs are from a biography of Abraham Lincoln. Notice how the underlined signal words help you track the sequence of events in his life. (The words signaling major events are underlined twice.)

Abraham Lincoln was born <u>in 1809</u> in Kentucky. His family moved to Indiana <u>in 1816</u>, where his mother died <u>two years later</u>.

<u>In 1830</u> Abraham and his family moved to Illinois. <u>While he was there</u>, Abraham worked as a clerk, a postmaster, and a county surveyor. <u>Then</u> he studied law and grammar.

<u>In 1842</u> Abraham married Mary Todd. <u>In 1860</u> he was elected President of the United States. <u>Three years later</u> he gave the Emancipation Proclamation, stating that all slaves would be free.

<u>In 1865</u> Abraham Lincoln was shot <u>while</u> watching a play at Ford's Theater. He died <u>several hours later</u>.

- If you wanted to show the sequence of the major events described above, you could put them on a **time line**. It would look like this:

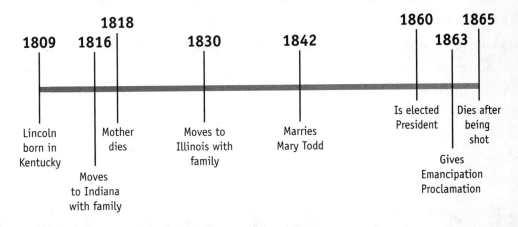

L. Frank Baum (Part 1)

by Carol Greene

Now use what you've learned to track the events in Part 1 of L. Frank Baum's biography. Notice the underlined signal words. They will help make the sequence clearer.

L. Frank Baum was a real person. He lived <u>from 1856 to 1919</u>. Frank wrote many books for children, including The Wonderful Wizard of Oz. *This is his story.*

Chapter 1

Scary Things and Secret Places

There it hung in the field, big and **spooky** and still. But wait! It moved! It was getting down from its post. Its long, long legs brought it closer, closer. It was going to get him!

Little Frank Baum woke up screaming. He'd had the **nightmare** again, the **scarecrow** nightmare.

"He reads too many **fairy tales**," said Frank's parents. "And he's not very healthy."

Frank *did* love fairy tales and he *wasn't* healthy. He had angina pectoris, a heart problem that made his chest hurt.

But Frank still had fun with his brothers and sisters. They lived on a farm, Rose Lawn, near Syracuse, New York. The children played croquet, baseball, and other games. They had friends over and went for carriage rides. They didn't even have to leave Rose Lawn to go to school. Mr. and Mrs. Baum hired teachers to come to them.

Frank couldn't play rough games because of his heart. But his mind got plenty of exercise. Frank liked to hide in secret places with his toys and **make-believe** friends. There he made up stories. He wanted to write fairy tales someday. But Frank knew how much **witches** and **goblins** scared him. So he promised himself that he wouldn't put scary things in *his* tales.

Frank didn't keep that promise.

Chapter 2

From School to Axle Grease

<u>When Frank was twelve</u>, his doctor said he could go away to boarding school. Frank's parents chose Peekskill Academy in Peekskill, New York.

Peekskill was a military school. Boys there learned to march and shoot a gun. They played rough games.

Frank hated it. He hated always being busy. He hated the way teachers hit students. He hated the rough games and the guns and the marching.

Frank stayed at Peekskill <u>for two long years</u>. <u>Then</u> something happened. No one knows just what. Maybe Frank had a heart attack. Maybe he just fainted. But Frank's parents let him come home <u>at last</u>.

<u>For his fourteenth birthday</u>, Frank's father gave him a little printing press. It was the perfect gift.

Frank and his brother Harry started a newspaper for their neighborhood. <u>Then</u>, <u>when Frank was seventeen</u>, he started another paper and a magazine for stamp collectors.

<u>Later</u>, Frank raised fancy chickens with his father and Harry. So he started a magazine about raising chickens.

⬣ **Stop here for the Strategy Break.**

Strategy Break

If you were to show the major events described in this biography so far, your time line might look like this:

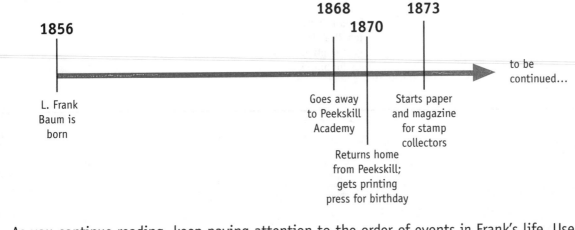

As you continue reading, keep paying attention to the order of events in Frank's life. Use the signal words to help you. At the end of this selection, you will continue the time line on your own.

➡️ **Go on reading.**

As time passed, Frank went from one job to another. He was an actor for a while. Then he began to write a musical.

Frank was still working on the musical when he met Maud Gage. Soon he wanted to marry her.

Maud's mother said Maud would be "a darned fool" to marry Frank. Maud decided to be "a darned fool." They were married in 1882.

For a while, Frank acted in his musical and he and Maud traveled. Then they rented a house in Syracuse and Frank sold axle grease for wagon wheels.

In 1883, Frank, Jr., was born. Robert came along in 1886. Now Frank was a family man. ●

Strategy Follow-up

Now continue the time line. Use a separate sheet of paper if necessary. Fill in only the major events. In Lesson 8 you will continue the time line as you read Part 2 of L. Frank Baum's biography.

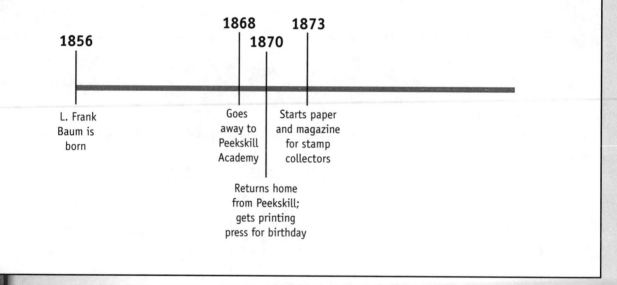

✓Personal Checklist

Read each question and put a check (✓) in the correct box.

1. How well did Building Background help you understand Frank's fear of scary creatures?
   - ☐ 3 (extremely well)
   - ☐ 2 (fairly well)
   - ☐ 1 (not well)

2. In the Vocabulary Builder, how many vocabulary words were you able to use in the scary story that you wrote?
   - ☐ 3 (6–7 words)
   - ☐ 2 (3–5 words)
   - ☐ 1 (0–2 words)

3. In the Strategy Follow-up, how well were you able to organize the major events of Frank's life on the time line?
   - ☐ 3 (extremely well)
   - ☐ 2 (fairly well)
   - ☐ 1 (not well)

4. How well do you understand why Frank didn't like Peekskill Academy?
   - ☐ 3 (extremely well)
   - ☐ 2 (fairly well)
   - ☐ 1 (not well)

5. How well do you understand why a printing press was the perfect gift for Frank?
   - ☐ 3 (extremely well)
   - ☐ 2 (fairly well)
   - ☐ 1 (not well)

Vocabulary Check

Look back at the work you did in the Vocabulary Builder. Then answer each question by circling the correct letter.

1. Which of the following is *not* a scary creature?
   - a. nightmare
   - b. goblin
   - c. witch

2. Frank dreamed about a big, spooky scarecrow. What does *spooky* mean?
   - a. funny
   - b. ugly
   - c. scary

3. Which word describes the stories that Frank wanted to write when he grew up?
   - a. fairy tales
   - b. nightmares
   - c. goblins

4. Frank liked to play with his make-believe friends. What does *make-believe* mean?
   - a. real
   - b. not real
   - c. true

5. Which vocabulary word were you able to figure out by using the context clue "woke up screaming"?
   - a. scarecrow
   - b. nightmare
   - c. spooky

Add the numbers that you just checked to get your Personal Checklist score. Fill in your score here. Then turn to page 201 and transfer your score onto Graph 1.

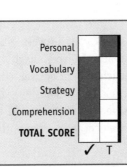

Check your answers with your teacher. Give yourself 1 point for each correct answer, and fill in your Vocabulary score here. Then turn to page 201 and transfer your score onto Graph 1.

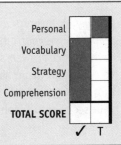

Strategy Check

Review the time line that you worked on in the Strategy Follow-up. Then answer these questions:

1. According to the time line, what happened in 1868?
   a. L. Frank Baum was born.
   b. Frank went away to Peekskill Academy.
   c. Frank and Maud's son Robert was born.

2. How old was Frank when he married Maud Gage?
   a. about 26 years old
   b. about 17 years old
   c. about 30 years old

3. When was Frank, Jr., born?
   a. before Robert was born
   b. when Robert was born
   c. after Robert was born

4. How many years had Frank and Maud been married when Robert was born?
   a. about 1 year
   b. about 2 years
   c. about 4 years

5. Which phrase is *not* an example of signal words?
   a. when Frank was twelve
   b. no one knows just what
   c. for a while

Comprehension Check

Review the selection if necessary. Then answer these questions:

1. Why wasn't little Frank Baum very healthy?
   a. because he had a heart problem
   b. because he read too many fairy tales
   c. because he had too many nightmares

2. How did Frank's mind get plenty of exercise when he was young?
   a. He played rough games.
   b. He made up stories.
   c. He went for carriage rides.

3. Why was Frank unhappy at Peekskill Academy?
   a. because he couldn't play rough games
   b. because the teachers always hit him
   c. because it was rough and always busy

4. Which words describe Frank as a boy?
   a. loud and wild
   b. imaginative and quiet
   c. happy and unintelligent

5. Maud's mother said that Maud was "a darned fool" for marrying Frank. What does this suggest about Maud's mother's feelings toward Frank?
   a. She probably felt that Frank would make an excellent husband.
   b. She probably felt that Frank wouldn't make a very good husband.
   c. She probably felt that Frank was much too smart for Maud.

Check your answers with your teacher. Give yourself 1 point for each correct answer, and fill in your Strategy score here. Then turn to page 201 and transfer your score onto Graph 1.

Personal
Vocabulary
Strategy
Comprehension
TOTAL SCORE
✓ T

Check your answers with your teacher. Give yourself 1 point for each correct answer, and fill in your Comprehension score here. Then turn to page 201 and transfer your score onto Graph 1.

Personal
Vocabulary
Strategy
Comprehension
TOTAL SCORE

✓ T

Extending

Choose one or both of these activities:

PRODUCE A NEWSPAPER

Get together with a group of students and produce a newspaper about your class or school. You might:

- interview and write an article about your teacher

- report on a "student of the week"

- report on the food in the cafeteria

- create a cartoon

- include a photo of your class or an important school event

- report the results of a survey about a topic that's important to your class or school

See the resources listed on this page for other ideas. Create your newspaper on a computer and make photocopies of it. Or paste your articles and photos onto a piece of heavy paper or cardboard. Then share your newspaper with the class or school.

CREATE A TIME LINE OF YOUR OWN LIFE

Create a time line that tracks the major events in your own life so far. Include the year you were born, the year you started school, and any other major events. If you'd like, place your time line on a wall in your room. Continue adding events to the time line as they happen.

Resources

Book

Bentley, Nancy, and Donna Guthrie. *The Young Journalist's Book: How to Write and Produce Your Own Newspaper.* Millbrook Press, 1998.

Web Sites

http://crayon.net
This site helps you create your own newspaper with step-by-step instructions.

http://www.halcyon.com/piglet
This Web site is a guide to the land of Oz and its inhabitants, as created by L. Frank Baum and the illustrators and writers who have contributed to the site.

L. Frank Baum (Part 2)

Building Background

From "L. Frank Baum" (Part 1):

*As time passed, Frank went from one job to another. He was an actor for a while. Then he began to write a **musical.***

Frank was still working on the musical when he met Maud Gage. Soon he wanted to marry her.

Maud's mother said Maud would be "a darned fool" to marry Frank. Maud decided to be "a darned fool." They were married in 1882.

For a while, Frank acted in his musical, and he and Maud traveled. Then they rented a house in Syracuse, and Frank sold axle grease for wagon wheels.

In 1883, Frank, Jr., was born. Robert came along in 1886. Now Frank was a family man.

adventures

cyclone

earned

musical

operation

publisher

shooed

Vocabulary Builder

1. Each of the sentences on page 77 contains a boldfaced vocabulary word. As you read each sentence, first use context clues to figure out what the boldfaced word means. Then decide whether it is used correctly or not.

2. If the boldfaced word is used correctly, write a **C** on the line. If it is not used correctly, write an **I** on the line.

_____ a. I have **adventures** in the park when nothing special happens.

_____ b. The **cyclone** blew through the town, tearing up the trees.

_____ c. Jon **earned** his money by not working and watching television.

_____ d. There won't be any songs in this movie because it's a **musical**.

_____ e. She needs an **operation** because her heart is strong and healthy.

_____ f. The **publisher** showed them the books that he had printed.

_____ g. Mother **shooed** away the birds by waving her arms.

3. Save your work. You will use it again in the Vocabulary Check.

Strategy Builder

Reading a Biography

- In Lesson 7 you learned that a **biography** tells the story of a real person's life, and is written by someone else.

- As you discovered while reading Part 1 of L. Frank Baum's biography, the events in Frank's life were told in the **sequence**, or time order, in which they happened. You used the **signal words** that the author provided to keep track of that sequence. Some of those signal words—such as _then, later, for a while,_ and _at last_—helped you link one smaller event to the next. However, other signal words such as _When Frank was twelve_ or _in 1883,_ helped you track the major events in Frank's life.

- Keep looking for signal words as you read Part 2 of L. Frank Baum's biography. They will help you as you continue the time line that you began in Lesson 7.

L. Frank Baum (Part 2)

by Carol Greene

Chapter 3

Oz!

The next few years brought more moves and changes. First the Baums moved to Aberdeen, South Dakota, and opened a store. When the store closed, Frank ran a newspaper. Two more little boys, Harry and Kenneth, were born.

At last, the Baums moved to Chicago and Frank found a job selling dishes. But when he wasn't working, he loved to tell stories to his boys and their friends. Sometimes Frank made up stories about the characters in nursery rhymes.

Maud's mother thought those stories were good. She made Frank send them to a **publisher**. *Mother Goose in Prose* came out in 1897.

Then Frank's heart began to bother him again. His doctor said he shouldn't sell dishes anymore. So Frank wrote full-time.

Frank had a whole stack of funny poems he had written. He showed them to an artist, William Denslow. Denslow drew pictures to go with the poems, and *Father Goose, His Book,* came out in 1899.

Till then, most pictures in children's books were in black and white. But Frank and Denslow wanted color on every page. That was a good idea. *Father Goose* became the best-selling children's book of the year.

One day, Frank was telling a story to his boys and their friends. It was about a girl who is blown by a **cyclone** to a magic land.

All at once, something clicked in Frank's mind. He **shooed** the children away and began to write as fast as he could.

The story was about Dorothy and her dog, Toto, who traveled to the land of Oz. They had **adventures** with the Scarecrow, the Tin Woodsman, and the Cowardly Lion. Denslow painted pictures with plenty of color, and in 1900, *The Wonderful Wizard of Oz* came out.

"Where did you get the name 'Oz'?" people asked Frank. He said he was looking at his file drawers. The first was labeled A–G. The second said H–N. The third said O–Z and that's where he got the name.

That *might* be true. Or it might be another story that Frank made up. Sometimes he couldn't stop himself.

Frank didn't want to put scary things in his story, and he didn't think he had. But some children thought the cyclone and the Wicked Witch of the West were pretty scary. They didn't mind, though. They loved the book. *The Wonderful Wizard of Oz* was the best-selling children's book for 1900.

⬣ **Stop here for the Strategy Break.**

Strategy Break

Now continue the time line that you began in Lesson 7. First, copy the time line below onto a large sheet of paper. Then add the major events from the part of Frank's biography that you just read. Leave room at the end of your time line. You will finish it in the Strategy Follow-up.

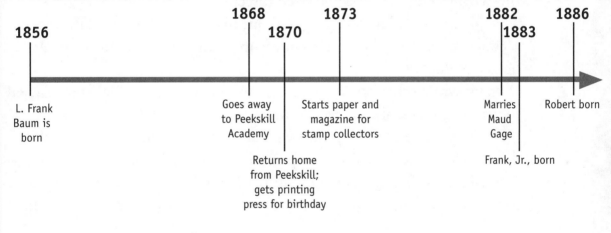

As you read the end of this biography, continue to track the events in Frank Baum's life. Use the signal words to help you. When you get to the Strategy Follow-up, you will finish the time line.

Go on reading.

Chapter 4

More Oz

Soon Frank and Denslow began work on a musical of *The Wizard of Oz*. Paul Tietjens wrote the music. The three men worked at Frank's house. They sang, danced, and acted silly. The musical was good, though, and did well.

That was fine with Frank's readers. But they really wanted more books about Oz. And Frank wouldn't write them. He thought he'd told the whole story of Oz. So he wrote books about other magic lands. He even wrote a book about Santa Claus.

But, at last, Frank gave in and wrote *The Marvelous Land of Oz*. Some characters from the first book are in it. So is a wonderful new character, the Woggle-Bug. It's a people-sized insect.

Frank and Denslow had a fight about money. So John Neill drew the pictures for the new book. He ended up doing the art for thirteen Oz books in all.

Frank wrote other books too. Some weren't very good. But they **earned** money and Frank always needed money.

The boys were grown up, so Frank and Maud could travel—and they did. In 1906, they went to Europe and northern Africa.

But Frank still couldn't stop writing Oz books, even when he wanted to. Almost every year, he wrote a new one. And still his readers cried, "More!"

Chapter 5

Ozcot

In 1911, Frank and Maud built a house in Hollywood, California. Frank called it Ozcot. Ozcot was big and comfortable. Outside were a huge bird-cage, a chicken yard, goldfish ponds, and a beautiful garden.

Frank loved that garden. There he dug and planted. He wrote books there too. Sometimes children visited him in his garden and Frank told them stories.

But as time went by, Frank's health grew worse. He had to have an **operation**. That made his heart weaker. Soon he had to stay in bed.

On May 5, 1919, Frank Baum had a stroke. It took away most of his power to speak. But on May 6, he opened his eyes for just a moment. "Now we can cross the Shifting Sands," he said. Then, quietly, he died.

Twenty years after Frank died, MGM brought out its film, *The Wizard of Oz*. Frank would have loved it.

Today, some adults say the Oz books are no good. But children know better and Frank wrote for *them*. "I would much rather be your story-teller," he wrote to his young readers, ". . . than to be the President." ●

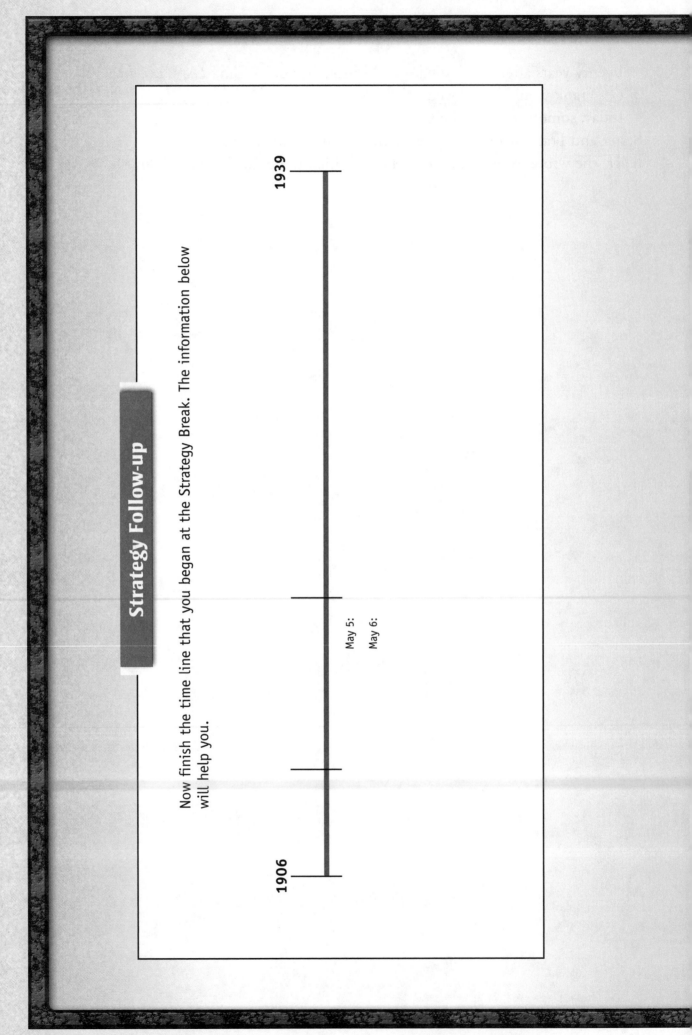

Strategy Follow-up

Now finish the time line that you began at the Strategy Break. The information below will help you.

1906

May 5:

May 6:

1939

✓Personal Checklist

Read each question and put a check (✓) in the correct box.

1. After reading this biography, how well would you be able to tell someone about L. Frank Baum's life?
   - ☐ 3 (extremely well)
   - ☐ 2 (fairly well)
   - ☐ 1 (not well)

2. How well do you understand why Frank didn't mind if adults didn't like his books?
   - ☐ 3 (extremely well)
   - ☐ 2 (fairly well)
   - ☐ 1 (not well)

3. You read in Building Background that Maud's mother thought Maud was "a darned fool" for marrying Frank. How well do you understand why she might have felt that way?
   - ☐ 3 (extremely well)
   - ☐ 2 (fairly well)
   - ☐ 1 (not well)

4. In the Vocabulary Builder, how well were you able to figure out if the boldfaced words were used correctly?
   - ☐ 3 (extremely well)
   - ☐ 2 (fairly well)
   - ☐ 1 (not well)

5. How well were you able to complete the time lines in the Strategy Break and Follow-up?
   - ☐ 3 (extremely well)
   - ☐ 2 (fairly well)
   - ☐ 1 (not well)

Vocabulary Check

Look back at the work you did in the Vocabulary Builder. Then answer each question by circling the correct letter.

1. Which context clue helped you know that *cyclone* was used correctly?
   a. when nothing special happened
   b. blew through the town, tearing up the trees
   c. by not working and watching television

2. Which vocabulary word were you able to figure out using the context clue "waving her arms"?
   a. shooed
   b. earned
   c. comfortable

3. Which word were you able to figure out from the clue "all the books that he had printed"?
   a. operation
   b. adventures
   c. publisher

4. How did you know that the word *musical* was used incorrectly?
   a. because a musical is a movie with no music in it
   b. because a musical is a movie that has music in it
   c. because movies are never musicals

5. How did you know that the word *adventures* was used incorrectly?
   a. because adventures are exciting experiences
   b. because adventures never happen in parks
   c. because adventures are nothing special

Add the numbers that you just checked to get your Personal Checklist score. Fill in your score here. Then turn to page 201 and transfer your score onto Graph 1.

Check your answers with your teacher. Give yourself 1 point for each correct answer, and fill in your Vocabulary score here. Then turn to page 201 and transfer your score onto Graph 1.

Strategy Check

Review the time lines that you worked on in this lesson. Then answer these questions:

1. When was Frank's book *The Wonderful Wizard of Oz* published?
   a. 1897
   b. 1899
   c. 1900

2. How old was Frank when *Father Goose, His Book* was published?
   a. about 41
   b. about 43
   c. about 46

3. Which years on your time lines list two events each?
   a. 1856 and 1897
   b. 1906 and 1911
   c. 1870 and 1919

4. When did Frank go to Europe with Maud?
   a. before *Father Goose, His Book* was published
   b. before they built Ozcot
   c. before *The Wonderful Wizard of Oz* was published

5. Which signal words helped you understand that the movie *The Wizard of Oz* came out in 1939?
   a. when he wasn't working
   b. at last
   c. twenty years after Frank died

Comprehension Check

Review the selection if necessary. Then answer these questions:

1. Who made Frank send his poems to a publisher?
   a. Maud
   b. his doctor
   c. Maud's mother

2. What happened when Frank told his children a story about a girl who was blown away by a cyclone?
   a. He wrote *The Wonderful Wizard of Oz*.
   b. He had a stroke and had to go into the hospital.
   c. He wrote *The Marvelous Land of Oz*.

3. Why didn't Frank want to write any more books about Oz?
   a. He thought he had told the whole story in *The Wonderful Wizard of Oz*.
   b. He decided that he wanted to write books for adults.
   c. He decided that he wanted to write only musicals.

4. What did Frank say just before he died?
   a. Nothing, since his stroke took away his power to speak.
   b. "Now we can cross the shifting sands."
   c. "I would much rather be your story-teller than to be the President."

5. Why didn't Frank care what adults thought of his books?
   a. He didn't like adults very much.
   b. He didn't want to be President.
   c. He wrote his books for children.

Check your answers with your teacher. Give yourself 1 point for each correct answer, and fill in your Strategy score here. Then turn to page 201 and transfer your score onto Graph 1.

Personal
Vocabulary
Strategy
Comprehension
TOTAL SCORE
✓ T

Check your answers with your teacher. Give yourself 1 point for each correct answer, and fill in your Comprehension score here. Then turn to page 201 and transfer your score onto Graph 1.

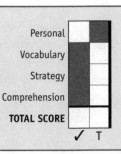

Personal
Vocabulary
Strategy
Comprehension
TOTAL SCORE
✓ T

Extending

Choose one or more of these activities.

WRITE AN OZ STORY

Write a short story about the land of Oz. You might include Dorothy, the Scarecrow, and other characters in your story. Or you might make up your own characters. If you'd like, you can send your short story to the first Web site listed on this page.

READ *THE WONDERFUL WIZARD OF OZ*

Read all or part of L. Frank Baum's *The Wonderful Wizard of Oz*. Then compare it to what you know about the movie, *The Wizard of Oz*. How are they different? How are they alike? Which do you like better? Why? Write a paragraph or two to answer these questions.

MAKE AN OZ COSTUME

Make a costume based on one of the characters in *The Wizard of Oz*. Then organize an "Oz Party." Invite people to come to your party dressed as their favorite Oz characters. Serve treats and drinks that might be found in the land of Oz.

Resources

Books

Bauer, Marion Dane. *Our Stories: A Fiction Workshop for Young Authors*. Clarion Books, 1996.

Baum, L. Frank. *The Wonderful Wizard of Oz*. Dover, 1960.

Hershberger, Priscilla, and Kim Solga. *Make Costumes for Creative Play*. North Light Books, 1992.

Web Site

http://www.stonesoup.com
Stone Soup, a magazine by young writers and artists, has stories, poems, book reviews, author readings, and artwork by kids 8–13 years old.

http://www.fabriclink.com/closet.html
This site includes links to lots of sites with ideas for making costumes.

Video/DVD

The Wizard of Oz (1939). Warner Studio, 1999.

The Cowardly Lion

Building Background

The selection you are about to read is a chapter from *The Wonderful Wizard of Oz* by L. Frank Baum. You remember that the movie *The Wizard of Oz* is based on Baum's book. You probably also remember that each character in the movie is going to see the Wizard to ask him for something. If you had a chance to ask the Wizard for something, what would it be? On the lines below, describe what thing, quality, or situation you would ask the Wizard for—and why.

_____

_____

_____

_____

astonished

bounded

companions

coward

heedless

journey

protect

strides

unbearable

Vocabulary Builder

1. The words in the margin are all from "The Cowardly Lion." Use what you already know about the words to answer the questions below. Write your answers on a separate sheet of paper.

2. If there are any questions that you can't answer, find the boldfaced vocabulary words in the selection and use context to figure out their meanings. If using context doesn't help, use a dictionary. Then try to answer the questions again.

   a. If Sarah has an **astonished** look on her face, does she look shocked or angry?

   b. If Eric **bounded** down the steps, would he be moving quickly or slowly?

   c. What are the names of your three best **companions**?

   d. If Tyra is brave and fearless, would she be a **coward**?

e. If Mason is **heedless** of the traffic as he crosses the street, is he careful?

f. If you could take a **journey** to anywhere in the world, where would you go?

g. What would **protect** you from the sun's harmful rays?

h. If Jessica is very tall, does she take long or short **strides** when she walks?

i. Which situation would be **unbearable**—a day at the beach in a bathing suit or a day at the beach in a fur coat?

3. Save your work. You will use it again in the Vocabulary Check.

Strategy Builder

Reading a Fantasy Story

- "The Cowardly Lion" is a type of fiction called fantasy. A **fantasy** is a make-believe story with one or more of these elements:

  —imaginary events that happen in imaginary settings, such as a magic kingdom, a strange planet, or a place in the past or future. Much of the movie *Star Wars* takes place in a made-up galaxy. The time of the movie is centuries into the future.

  —imaginary characters, such as elves, witches, or animals that talk. Some characters in a fantasy could exist in real life, but many other characters could not. Although fantasy characters are often similar to real people or animals, they also have characteristics that make them fantastical, or imaginary. For example, think about the robot R2D2 in *Star Wars*. Robots do exist in real life. However, R2D2 has many characteristics that make him a fantasy character.

- The following chart lists some of the characteristics that make R2D2 seem like both a real robot and an imaginary robot.

How R2D2 Seems Real	How R2D2 Seems Imaginary
• He's made of gears and metal parts. • He looks like a real robot. • He moves in a stiff, robotlike manner. • He breaks down and has to be fixed. • He can be programmed.	• He talks and thinks like a person (he has a mind of his own sometimes). • He has human feelings and emotions. • He's loyal to his friends. • He can be a pest sometimes.

The Cowardly Lion

from *The Wonderful Wizard of Oz*
by L. Frank Baum

As you read "The Cowardly Lion," apply what you learned about fantasy. In this first part, look for clues that tell you that this selection takes place in an imaginary setting.

All this time Dorothy and her **companions** had been walking through the thick woods. The road was still paved with yellow bricks, but these were much covered by dried branches and dead leaves from the trees, and the walking was not at all good.

There were few birds in this part of the forest, for birds love the open country where there is plenty of sunshine. But now and then there came a deep growl from some wild animal hidden among the trees. These sounds made the little girl's heart beat fast, for she did not know what made them; but Toto knew, and he walked close to Dorothy's side, and did not even bark in return.

"How long will it be," the child asked of the Tin Woodman, "before we are out of the forest?"

"I cannot tell," was the answer, "for I have never been to the Emerald City. But my father went there once, when I was a boy, and he said it was a long **journey** through a dangerous country, although nearer to the city where Oz dwells the country is beautiful. But I am not afraid so long as I have my oilcan, and nothing can hurt the Scarecrow, while you bear upon your forehead the mark of the Good Witch's kiss, and that will **protect** you from harm."

"But Toto!" said the girl anxiously. "What will protect him?"

"We must protect him ourselves if he is in danger," replied the Tin Woodman.

Just as he spoke there came from the forest a terrible roar, and the next moment a great Lion **bounded** into the road. With one blow of his paw he sent the Scarecrow spinning over and over to the edge of the road, and then he struck at the Tin Woodman with his sharp claws. But, to the Lion's surprise, he could make no impression on the tin, although the Woodman fell over in the road and lay still.

⬡ **Stop here for the Strategy Break.**

Strategy Break

Although the author doesn't say *when* the action takes place, he does give some clues about *where* it takes place. The following chart lists some ways in which the setting seems both real and imaginary.

How the Setting Seems Real	How the Setting Seems Imaginary
• It's in a thick forest. • The forest has birds and other animals in it.	• The forest has a road paved with yellow bricks. • There is no such thing as an Emerald City or a land called Oz where a Wizard lives.

As you read the rest of this selection, focus on the Lion. Look for clues that tell you that he is a fantasy character.

 Go on reading to see what happens.

Little Toto, now that he had an enemy to face, ran barking toward the Lion, and the great beast had opened his mouth to bite the dog, when Dorothy, fearing Toto would be killed, and **heedless** of danger, rushed forward and slapped the Lion upon his nose as hard as she could, while she cried out:

"Don't you dare to bite Toto! You ought to be ashamed of yourself, a big beast like you, to bite a poor little dog!"

"I didn't bite him," said the Lion, as he rubbed his nose with his paw where Dorothy had hit it.

"No, but you tried to," she retorted. "You are nothing but a big coward."

"I know it," said the Lion, hanging his head in shame. "I've always known it. But how can I help it?"

"I don't know, I'm sure. To think of your striking a stuffed man, like the poor Scarecrow!"

"Is he stuffed?" asked the Lion in surprise, as he watched her pick up the Scarecrow and set him upon his feet, while she patted him into shape again.

"Of course he's stuffed," replied Dorothy, who was still angry.

"That's why he went over so easily," remarked the Lion. "It **astonished** me to see him whirl around so. Is the other one stuffed also?"

"No," said Dorothy, "he's made of tin." And she helped the Woodman up again.

"That's why he nearly blunted my claws," said the Lion. "When they scratched against the tin it made a cold shiver run down my back. What is that little animal you are so tender of?"

"He is my dog, Toto," answered Dorothy.

"Is he made of tin, or stuffed?" asked the Lion.

"Neither. He's a—a—a meat dog," said the girl.

"Oh! He's a curious animal and seems remarkably small, now that I look at him. No one would think of biting such a little thing except a **coward** like me," continued the Lion sadly.

"What makes you a coward?" asked Dorothy, looking at the great beast in wonder, for he was as big as a small horse.

"It's a mystery," replied the Lion. "I suppose I was born that way. All the other animals in the forest naturally expect me to be brave, for the Lion is everywhere thought to be the King of Beasts. I learned that if I roared very loudly every living thing was frightened and got out of my way. Whenever I've met a man I've been awfully scared. But I just roared at him, and he has always run away as fast as he could go. If the elephants and the tigers and the bears had ever tried to fight me, I should have run myself—I'm such a coward; but just as soon as they hear me roar they all try to get away from me, and of course I let them go."

"But that isn't right. The King of Beasts shouldn't be a coward," said the Scarecrow.

"I know it," returned the Lion, wiping a tear from his eye with the tip of his paw. "It is my great sorrow, and makes my life very unhappy. But whenever there is danger, my heart begins to beat fast."

"Perhaps you have a heart disease," said the Tin Woodman.

"It may be," said the Lion.

"If you have," continued the Tin Woodman, "you ought to be glad, for it proves you have a heart. For my part, I have no heart, so I cannot have heart disease."

"Perhaps," said the Lion thoughtfully, "if I had no heart I should not be a coward."

"Have you brains?" asked the Scarecrow.

"I suppose so. I've never looked to see," replied the Lion.

"I am going to the Great Oz to ask him to give me some," remarked the Scarecrow, "for my head is stuffed with straw."

"And I am going to ask him to give me a heart," said the Woodman.

"And I am going to ask him to send Toto and me back to Kansas," added Dorothy.

"Do you think Oz could give me courage?" asked the Cowardly Lion.

"Just as easily as he could give me brains," said the Scarecrow.

"Or give me a heart," said the Tin Woodman.

"Or send me back to Kansas," said Dorothy.

"Then, if you don't mind, I'll go with you," said the Lion, "for my life is simply **unbearable** without a bit of courage."

"You will be very welcome," answered Dorothy, "for you will help to keep away the other wild beasts. It seems to me they must be more cowardly than you are if they allow you to scare them so easily."

"They really are," said the Lion, "but that doesn't make me any braver, and as long as I know myself to be a coward I shall be unhappy."

So once more the little company set off upon the journey, the Lion walking with stately **strides** at Dorothy's side. Toto did not approve this new comrade at first, for he could not forget how nearly he had been crushed between the Lion's great jaws. But after a time he became more at ease, and presently Toto and the Cowardly Lion had grown to be good friends.

During the rest of that day there was no other adventure to mar the peace of their journey. Once, indeed, the Tin Woodman stepped upon a beetle that was crawling along the road, and killed the poor little thing. This made the Tin Woodman very unhappy, for he was always careful not to hurt any living creature; and as he walked along he wept several tears of sorrow and regret. These tears ran slowly down his face and over the hinges of his jaw, and there they rusted. When Dorothy presently asked him a question the Tin Woodman could not open his mouth, for his jaws were tightly rusted together. He became greatly frightened at this and made many motions to Dorothy to relieve him, but she could not understand. The Lion was also puzzled to know what was wrong. But the Scarecrow seized the oilcan from Dorothy's basket and oiled the Woodman's jaws, so that after a few moments he could talk as well as before.

"This will serve me a lesson," said he, "to look where I step. For if I should kill another bug or beetle I should surely cry again, and crying rusts my jaws so that I cannot speak."

Thereafter he walked very carefully, with his eyes on the road, and when he saw a tiny ant toiling by he would step over it, so as not to harm it. The Tin Woodman knew very well he had no heart, and therefore he took great care never to be cruel or unkind to anything.

"You people with hearts," he said, "have something to guide you, and need never do wrong; but I have no heart, and so I must be very careful. When Oz gives me a heart, of course I needn't mind so much." ●

Strategy Follow-up

On the chart below, list clues from the selection that make the Lion seem like a fantasy character.

How the Lion Seems Real	How the Lion Seems Imaginary

✓Personal Checklist

Read each question and put a check (✓) in the correct box.

1. How well do you understand why the Cowardly Lion wants to ask the Wizard for courage?
   - ☐ 3 (extremely well)
   - ☐ 2 (fairly well)
   - ☐ 1 (not well)

2. How well do you understand why the Tin Woodman cries when he steps on a beetle?
   - ☐ 3 (extremely well)
   - ☐ 2 (fairly well)
   - ☐ 1 (not well)

3. In Building Background, how well were you able to describe what you would ask the Wizard for, and why?
   - ☐ 3 (extremely well)
   - ☐ 2 (fairly well)
   - ☐ 1 (not well)

4. In the Vocabulary Builder, how many questions were you able to answer by the time you finished this selection?
   - ☐ 3 (7–9 questions)
   - ☐ 2 (4–6 questions)
   - ☐ 1 (0–3 questions)

5. In the Strategy Follow-up, how well were you able to list clues that make the Cowardly Lion seem both real and imaginary?
   - ☐ 3 (extremely well)
   - ☐ 2 (fairly well)
   - ☐ 1 (not well)

Vocabulary Check

Look back at the work you did in the Vocabulary Builder. Then answer each question by circling the correct letter.

1. Who are Dorothy's traveling companions in this selection?
   a. the Tin Woodman, Oz, Toto, the Scarecrow, and the Lion
   b. the Tin Woodman, Toto, the Scarecrow, and the Lion
   c. the Tin Woodman, the Good Witch, the Scarecrow, and the Lion

2. As the other characters were walking along, the Lion suddenly bounded onto the road. What does *bounded* mean?
   a. jumped
   b. fell
   c. tiptoed

3. It astonished the Lion to see the Scarecrow whirl around when he hit him. What does *astonished* mean?
   a. saddened
   b. scared
   c. shocked

4. Which vocabulary word were you able to figure out from the context clue "rushed forward and slapped the Lion upon his nose"?
   a. bounded
   b. heedless
   c. astonished

5. Which vocabulary word were you able to figure out from the context clues "the Lion walking" and "at Dorothy's side"?
   a. strides
   b. protect
   c. journey

Add the numbers that you just checked to get your Personal Checklist score. Fill in your score here. Then turn to page 201 and transfer your score onto Graph 1.

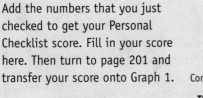

Check your answers with your teacher. Give yourself 1 point for each correct answer, and fill in your Vocabulary score here. Then turn to page 201 and transfer your score onto Graph 1.

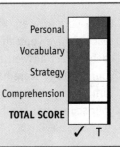

Strategy Check

Review the chart you completed in the Strategy Follow-up. Also review the rest of the selection. Then answer these questions:

1. Which character in "The Cowardly Lion" could exist in real life?
   a. Scarecrow
   b. Dorothy
   c. Cowardly Lion

2. What is one of the Lion's realistic features?
   a. He has a terrible roar.
   b. He talks.
   c. He's cries when he's unhappy.

3. Which feature makes the Lion a fantasy character?
   a. He has a deep growl.
   b. He talks.
   c. He's very large and strong.

4. How do you know that the Tin Woodman is a fantasy character?
   a. There is no such thing as a man made of tin.
   b. A real tin man wouldn't cry.
   c. A real tin man wouldn't need to be oiled.

5. Why do you think Frank Baum gave the Lion, the Scarecrow, and the Tin Woodman human characteristics?
   a. to make readers want to be just like them
   b. to make readers dislike them
   c. to help readers like and understand them

Comprehension Check

Review the selection if necessary. Then answer these questions:

1. What will protect Dorothy from harm as she walks through the woods?
   a. her oilcan
   b. the Good Witch's kiss
   c. Toto

2. What happens when the Lion hits the Scarecrow?
   a. The Lion's blow has no effect on the Scarecrow.
   b. The Scarecrow gets mad and hits the Lion back.
   c. The Scarecrow goes spinning over to the edge of the road.

3. How does the Lion frighten other creatures?
   a. He doesn't—other creatures know he's a coward.
   b. He roars very loudly at them.
   c. He chases them and tells them he'll eat them.

4. Why might the Tin Woodman wish he had heart disease?
   a. It would prove he had a heart.
   b. It would prove he had brains.
   c. It would prove he had courage.

5. Why does the Tin Woodman cry as he walks along the road?
   a. Dorothy slaps him.
   b. He steps upon a beetle.
   c. He wants to get home to Kansas.

Check your answers with your teacher. Give yourself 1 point for each correct answer, and fill in your Strategy score here. Then turn to page 201 and transfer your score onto Graph 1.

Personal
Vocabulary
Strategy
Comprehension
TOTAL SCORE
✓ T

Check your answers with your teacher. Give yourself 1 point for each correct answer, and fill in your Comprehension score here. Then turn to page 201 and transfer your score onto Graph 1.

Personal
Vocabulary
Strategy
Comprehension
TOTAL SCORE
✓ T

Extending

Choose one or both of these activities:

WRITE A JOURNAL ENTRY

Imagine that you are on your way to see the Wizard of Oz. Write a journal entry or two describing your adventures on the Yellow Brick Road. You might describe the creatures you meet along the road. Or you might tell what happens when you see the Wizard.

PERFORM "THE COWARDLY LION"

Get together with other students in your class to perform "The Cowardly Lion." Decide who will play each character. Then use the dialog in the story to figure out what everyone's lines will be. Rehearse your performance until everyone feels comfortable. Then perform the story for your class. If possible, use simple props and costumes.

Resources

Books

Baum, L. Frank. *Little Wizard Stories of Oz.* William Morrow, 1994.

————. *The Marvelous Land of Oz.* Books of Wonder. Harper Trophy, 2001.

Thompson, Ruth Plumly. *The Cowardly Lion of Oz.* Wonderful Oz Books. Ballantine Books, 1995.

Web Site

http://www.fabriclink.com/Closet.html
This site includes links to sites with ideas for making costumes.

The Big Balloon Race (Part 1)

aeronaut

aloft

hissed

passenger

scraped

spread

stowaway

swooped

CLIPBOARD

aeronaut

aloft

hissed

passenger

Building Background

The story you will read in this lesson and in Lesson 11 is based on a real-life family. Carl Myers was an inventor and a balloon maker. His wife Carlotta was a balloonist. Carlotta lived from 1849 to 1932. She was the best-known balloonist in America during the 1880s. She made more trips in hot air balloons than any other balloonist of her time. Carl made balloons for Carlotta at their home, called Balloon Farm. Carl and Carlotta's daughter, Ariel, also became a balloonist. She, too, flew in balloons made by her father.

Vocabulary Builder

1. Read the words in the margin. They are from Part 1 of *The Big Balloon Race*.

2. On the clipboards, write a meaning for each word. If a word has more than one meaning, predict how it might be used in the story and use that meaning.

3. Then use the vocabulary words and the title to help you predict what might happen in this story. Write your predictions on a separate sheet of paper. Use as many vocabulary words as possible.

4. Save your work. You will use it again in the Vocabulary Check.

CLIPBOARD

scraped

spread

stowaway

swooped

Strategy Builder

Mapping the Elements of Historical Fiction

- **Historical fiction** tells a made-up story based on real historical facts. *The Big Balloon Race* is historical fiction that describes events that could have happened to the Myers family. It also gives you an idea of what their real lives and adventures might have been like.

- An author of historical fiction often writes to inform and entertain readers. You may recall that authors write for one or more of these purposes: to **inform** (explain or describe something), to **entertain** (make readers laugh or smile), to **persuade** (try to get readers to agree with an opinion), or to **express** (share feelings or ideas about something).

- Historical fiction contains the same elements that you would find in any story. These elements include a **setting, characters,** and a sequence of events, or **plot**. The story you are about to read has been divided into two parts. You will use a story map to help you keep track of the elements in each part. Study the following story map. It lists and defines the elements that you should be looking for.

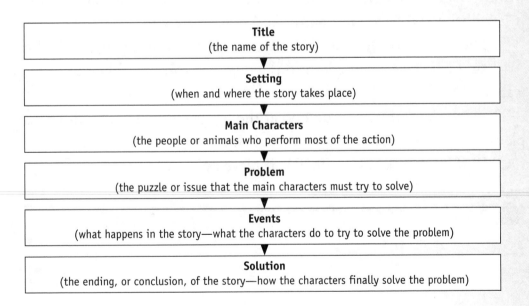

Title
(the name of the story)

Setting
(when and where the story takes place)

Main Characters
(the people or animals who perform most of the action)

Problem
(the puzzle or issue that the main characters must try to solve)

Events
(what happens in the story—what the characters do to try to solve the problem)

Solution
(the ending, or conclusion, of the story—how the characters finally solve the problem)

The Big Balloon Race (Part 1)

by Eleanor Coerr

As you read Part 1 of *The Big Balloon Race,* apply the strategies that you just learned. Keep track of the characters, events, and other elements in the story. You may want to underline them as you read.

It was the day of the big balloon race. Ariel got up early and hurried to her mother's room. "Please," she asked, "can I go up in the balloon with you?"

Carlotta the Great was putting on her blue dress with the fancy gold braid. "You are too young," she said, "and winning a race is hard work."

"But I can help," said Ariel.

Carlotta smiled. "You can help by riding in the buggy with your father to the finish line."

"Oh, thumps!" said Ariel. Sadly, she went outside.

Balloon Farm was a strange farm. In the yard half-filled balloons sat like giant mushrooms. People came from all over to buy balloons made by Mr. Myers. Ariel watched her father fold Carlotta's balloon, *Lucky Star.*

"I wish I could be an **aeronaut** like Mama," she said.

"When you are older," said Mr. Myers. "Now it is time to go." Carlotta, Ariel, and Mr. Myers climbed into the buggy. *Lucky Star* followed in a wagon.

There was a great whoop-de-doo at the fairgrounds. Thousands of people were there to see the balloon race. It was a big event in 1882. OOMPAH! OOMPAH! OOMPAH! played the band.

⬢ **Stop here for the Strategy Break.**

Strategy Break

If you stopped to create a story map for what you've read so far, it might look like this:

Title: *The Big Balloon Race* (Part 1)

▼

Setting: the day of the big balloon race, 1882

▼

Main Characters: Ariel, Carlotta the Great (Mrs. Myers), Mr. Myers

▼

Problem: Ariel wants to go up in the balloon, but her mother tells her she's too young.

▼

Events: 1. Carlotta prepares for the big race.
2. The family rides to the fairgrounds.

▼

To be continued . . .

Continue looking for story elements as you read the rest of Part 1. When you finish reading, you will continue the story map.

➡ **Go on reading to see what happens.**

Two balloons were already in the air. They were tied to the ground by long ropes. Acrobats swung from one basket to the other.

Lucky Star and its net were **spread** out on the ground. PFFFTTTTTT! Lighter-than-air hydrogen gas **hissed** into the balloon. It slowly grew until it was taller than the house on Balloon Farm. Twelve strong men held *Lucky Star* down.

Nearby, another balloon grew fat and tall. It was the *Flying Cloud,* a ball of bright colors. Its captain, Bernard the Brave, was the best gentleman aeronaut in America. Carlotta the Great was the best lady aeronaut. It would be a close race.

"I bet you will win," Ariel told her mother.

Carlotta gave her a kiss. "You can sit in the basket until it is time to go."

Ariel got inside the basket and talked to Harry the pigeon. Harry went on every flight. Sometimes he took messages from Carlotta to Balloon Farm.

The mayor began a long speech. He talked on and on. So Ariel climbed inside the Odds and Ends box. It was quieter there, and cozy and warm. Soon she was fast asleep.

Ariel did not hear the mayor's last words. "There is a south wind," he said, "so the finish line will be the other side of Devil's Punchbowl Lake." Ariel did not even hear the drums. TARUUUUUM!

The aeronauts stepped into their baskets. The crowd cheered. Mr. Myers waved to Carlotta. "Good luck!"

She waved her nobby sailor hat. "Hands off!" Carlotta ordered. The men let go of the ropes. With a jolt, *Lucky Star* took off.

Ariel woke up. "What happened?" she asked.

Carlotta stared. "Ariel! What have you done?" she cried. "We are **aloft**!"

Ariel looked over the side. Sure enough, they were off the ground. Below, someone yelled, "Stop! There is a **stowaway** in that basket!"

Mr. Myers waved his arms and shouted something. Ariel waved back. "Oooo!" she cried. "It's like being a bird."

She watched the crowd set out for the finish line. Some were in buggies, some were in wagons, and others were on fast horses.

A crosswind tugged at the balloon. WHOOOOSH! *Lucky Star* **swooped** away over a farm. Dogs barked and ran around in circles. Pigs squealed. Chickens squawked. A horse reared and galloped away. SCRUU-UUNCH! *Lucky Star*'s basket **scraped** the treetops.

"Can we go higher?" asked Ariel.

"The balloon and ballast are for only one **passenger**," said Carlotta. "You are extra weight."

She dropped one bag of sand over the side. Up went *Lucky Star*. The farm got smaller and smaller. It looked like a toy. Then it was gone. ●

Strategy Follow-up

On a separate sheet of paper, continue the story map for Part 1 of *The Big Balloon Race*. (You will read Part 2 in Lesson 11.) Parts of the events have been filled in for you.

Problem: Ariel wants to go up in the balloon, but her mother tells her she's too young.

▼

Events: 1. Carlotta prepares for the big race.

2. The family rides to the fairgrounds.

3. Carlotta tells Ariel

4. Ariel

5.

6. When Carlotta discovers Ariel,

▼

To be continued . . .

✓Personal Checklist

Read each question and put a check (✓) in the correct box.

1. How well do you understand how Ariel ends up taking part in the balloon race?
   - ☐ 3 (extremely well)
   - ☐ 2 (fairly well)
   - ☐ 1 (not well)

2. How well do you understand why Carlotta throws a bag of sand over the side of the balloon?
   - ☐ 3 (extremely well)
   - ☐ 2 (fairly well)
   - ☐ 1 (not well)

3. How well did the information in Building Background help you understand the characters and events in this selection?
   - ☐ 3 (extremely well)
   - ☐ 2 (fairly well)
   - ☐ 1 (not well)

4. In the Vocabulary Builder, how many words were you able to use in your prediction?
   - ☐ 3 (6–8 words)
   - ☐ 2 (3–5 words)
   - ☐ 1 (0–2 words)

5. How well were you able to complete the story map in the Strategy Follow-up?
   - ☐ 3 (extremely well)
   - ☐ 2 (fairly well)
   - ☐ 1 (not well)

Vocabulary Check

Look back at the work you did in the Vocabulary Builder. Then answer each question by circling the correct letter.

1. When a crosswind tugged at it, *Lucky Star* swooped away over a farm. What other object might swoop when tugged by wind?
   - a. a kite
   - b. a barn
   - c. a wagon

2. Ariel wishes she could be an aeronaut like her mother. What is another word for *aeronaut*?
   - a. stowaway
   - b. balloonist
   - c. passenger

3. In the story, Carlotta tells Ariel, "We are aloft!" Which context clue helped you figure out what *aloft* means?
   - a. Ariel woke up.
   - b. "What have you done?"
   - c. They were off the ground.

4. Someone on the ground calls Ariel a stowaway. What phrase most closely describes a stowaway?
   - a person who flies a balloon
   - b. person who travels in a balloon
   - c. person who hides on a balloon

5. What does the word *scraped* mean in the context of this story?
   - a. rubbed against
   - b. missed completely
   - c. knocked over

Add the numbers that you just checked to get your Personal Checklist score. Fill in your score here. Then turn to page 201 and transfer your score onto Graph 1.

Check your answers with your teacher. Give yourself 1 point for each correct answer, and fill in your Vocabulary score here. Then turn to page 201 and transfer your score onto Graph 1.

Strategy Check

Review the story map that you worked on in the Strategy Follow-up. Also review the selection if necessary. Then answer these questions:

1. Who is *not* a main character in Part 1 of *The Big Balloon Race?*

    a. Ariel

    b. Carlotta

    c. Bernard the Brave

2. On the story map, which sentence could you have listed for Event 5?

    a. The race begins, and Carlotta's balloon rises.

    b. The race begins, but Carlotta's balloon doesn't rise.

    c. Carlotta drops a sandbag over the side of the basket.

3. What could you have written about Ariel in Event 4?

    a. Ariel arrives with her parents at the fairgrounds.

    b. Ariel falls asleep during the mayor's long speech.

    c. Ariel watches her father fold *Lucky Star.*

4. When does Carlotta discover that Ariel is in *Lucky Star's* basket?

    a. while the mayor is speaking

    b. after *Lucky Star* is aloft

    c. before *Lucky Star* is aloft

5. Which element will you be able to add to the story map only after you've read Part 2 of this story?

    a. the setting

    b. the problem

    c. the conclusion

Comprehension Check

Review the story if necessary. Then answer these questions:

1. Why can't Ariel go up in the balloon with her mother?

    a. Ariel doesn't want to work hard.

    b. Ariel is afraid of flying.

    c. Ariel is too young.

2. What do the acrobats do at the fairgrounds?

    a. They hold *Lucky Star* on the ground.

    b. They swing from one balloon basket to another.

    c. They help fill the balloons with gas.

3. Why does the mayor's speech put Ariel to sleep?

    a. The speech is very short.

    b. The speech is very interesting.

    c. The speech is very long.

4. When *Lucky Star* first takes off, why does it fly so low to the ground?

    a. It is not meant to carry more than one person.

    b. Carlotta wants to land so Ariel can get out.

    c. Carlotta throws too much sand over the side of the basket.

5. What do you think was the author's main purpose for writing this story?

    a. to persuade her readers to take part in balloon races

    b. to inform her readers about a historical balloon race

    c. to express her opinions about balloon races

Check your answers with your teacher. Give yourself 1 point for each correct answer, and fill in your Strategy score here. Then turn to page 201 and transfer your score onto Graph 1.

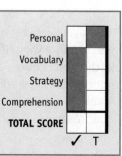

Check your answers with your teacher. Give yourself 1 point for each correct answer, and fill in your Comprehension score here. Then turn to page 201 and transfer your score onto Graph 1.

Extending

Choose one or both of these activities:

DRAW PICTURES OF STORY ELEMENTS

Using your story map, draw several pictures that show the characters, setting, problem, and events in Part 1 of *The Big Balloon Race.* If you need help with your drawing, see the resources listed on this page.

WRITE A REPORT ABOUT BALLOONING

Find out more about the history of ballooning. Also, research famous balloonists. Find out about the first team to fly around the world in a balloon. Report your findings to your class. If possible, bring in pictures of historic and modern hot air balloons. If you have access to the Internet, you might check the Web site listed on this page.

Resources

Books

Ames, Lee J. *Draw 50 Airplanes, Aircraft and Spacecraft.* Bt Bound, 1999.

Solga, Kim. *Draw!* Art and Activities. Hodder & Stoughton Children's Division, 1993.

Web Site

http://www.pbs.org/wgbh/nova/balloon
This site contains information on the history of ballooning and on modern balloonists.

Learning New Words

Compound Words

VOCABULARY

From Lesson 6
• mountainside

From Lesson 7
• scarecrow

From Lesson 10
• stowaway

A compound word is made of two words put together. When L. Frank Baum was a boy, he used to have scary dreams about scarecrows. *Scarecrow* is made of the words *scare* and *crow*. A scarecrow is a doll or dummy that farmers use to scare crows and other birds away from their crops.

Fill in each blank with a compound word by combining a word from Row 1 with a word from Row 2.

| Row 1: | row | bed | air | day | head |
| Row 2: | room | boat | break | plane | line |

1. craft that flies in the sky = _____

2. title of a newspaper article = _____

3. place where one sleeps = _____

4. time when it gets light = _____

5. craft moved by oars = _____

Suffixes

From Lesson 8
• publisher

A suffix is a word part that is added to the end of a root word. When you add a suffix, you often change the root word's meaning and function. For example, the suffix *-ful* means "full of," so adding *-ful* to the noun *peace* changes it to an adjective meaning "full of peace."

-er

The suffix *-er* is a special kind of suffix. It turns a verb into a noun that means "a person who _____." In Part 2 of L. Frank Baum's biography, you learned that Frank's *publisher* was the person who published, or brought out, his books.

Now write the word that describes each person below.

1. a person who works hard   _____

2. a person who walks a lot   _____

3. a person who thinks deeply   _____

4. a person who views films or TV   _____

5. a person who builds houses   _____

Prefixes

A prefix is a word part that is added to the beginning of a root word. (*Pre-* means "before.") When you add a prefix, you often change the root word's meaning and function. For example, the prefix *un-* means "not," so adding *un-* to the root word *tied* changes *tied* to its antonym, *untied.*

Write the definition of each word, as well as a synonym of the word. The first one has been done for you.

1. unseen   not seen, invisible

2. unhealthy   _____

3. unclean   _____

4. untrue   _____

5. unhappy   _____

6. unkind   _____

Prefixes and Suffixes

Some root words have both a prefix *and* a suffix added to them. In Lesson 9 the Cowardly Lion says that his life is unbearable without courage. *Unbearable* is made up of the root word *bear* plus the prefix *un-* and the suffix *-able*. The root word *bear* means "put up with" or "handle." The suffix *-able* means "able to be_____ed." So *unbearable* means "*not* able to be handled."

Write the word that each definition describes.

1. not able to be printed   _____

2. not able to be reached   _____

3. not able to be watched   _____

4. not able to be touched   _____

5. not able to be delivered   _____

6. not able to be published   _____

VOCABULARY

From Lesson 9
- unbearable

From Lesson 9
- unbearable

The Big Balloon Race (Part 2)

Building Background

From *The Big Balloon Race* (Part 2):

. . . With a jolt, Lucky Star *took off.*

Ariel woke up. "What happened?" she asked.

Carlotta stared. "Ariel! What have you done?" she cried. "We are aloft!"

Ariel looked over the side. Sure enough, they were off the ground. Below, someone yelled, "Stop! There is a stowaway in that basket!"

Mr. Myers waved his arms and shouted something. Ariel waved back. "Oooo!" she cried. "It's like being a bird."

She watched the crowd set out for the finish line. Some were in buggies, some were in wagons, and others were on fast horses.

A crosswind tugged at the balloon. WHOOOOSH! Lucky Star *swooped away over a farm. Dogs barked and ran around in circles. Pigs squealed. Chickens squawked. A horse reared and galloped away. SCRUUUUNCH!* Lucky Star'*s basket scraped the treetops.*

"Can we go higher?" asked Ariel.

"The balloon and ballast are for only one passenger," said Carlotta. "You are extra weight."

She dropped one bag of sand over the side. Up went Lucky Star. *The farm got smaller and smaller. It looked like a toy. Then it was gone.*

What do you predict will happen to Ariel and her mother? As you read on, pay attention to the events and the solution. You will use them to finish the story map that you started in Lesson 10.

afloat

misty

netting

skimmed

snugly

soared

stared

victory

Vocabulary Builder

1. Each word in the margin has a base word, or root word. A **root word** is a complete word by itself. However, you can add other words or word parts to a root word to make new words. For example, *build* is a root word. You can add *re-*, *-er*, and *-ing* to *build* to make *rebuild*, *builder*, and *building*. Identifying the root word of an unfamiliar word can sometimes help you figure out the word's meaning.

2. On a separate sheet of paper, write the root word of each vocabulary word. Then use the root word to help you figure out and write the vocabulary word's meaning. If you have trouble with any of the words, find them in the story and use context clues. Or look them up in a dictionary.

3. Save your work. You will use it again in the Vocabulary Check.

Strategy Builder

Summarizing Events in a Story

- Sometimes when you read a long story, it helps to stop once in a while and summarize what you've read. When you **summarize**, you briefly describe the main elements of the story—its setting, main characters, and the events that have happened so far.

- Think back to Part 1 of *The Big Balloon Race*. If you were going to summarize what happened in Part 1, you could use your story map to help you. Your summary might look like this:

> ### *The Big Balloon Race,* Part 1
>
> This story takes place in 1882. Ariel's mother, Carlotta, is a famous aeronaut. She is going to take part in the big balloon race. Ariel wants to go up in her mother's balloon, but Carlotta tells her she's too young.
>
> Ariel and her mother and father ride out to the fairgrounds. Carlotta tells Ariel that she can sit in the balloon's basket until it's time for the race to start. During the mayor's speech, Ariel falls asleep.
>
> Just after *Lucky Star* takes off, Ariel wakes up. Her mother tells her that *Lucky Star* is built for only one passenger. To get rid of the weight that Ariel adds, Carlotta drops a bag of sand over the side. *Lucky Star* rises up and out of sight.

The Big Balloon Race (Part 2)

by Eleanor Coerr

As you read Part 2 of *The Big Balloon Race*, think about how you might summarize this story. Keep paying attention to the story elements as you read. They will help you with your summaries.

"Dear me!" said Carlotta. "An updraft is sucking us into that rain cloud." She pulled on the blue valve rope to let out some gas. *Lucky Star* did not fall.

Ariel **stared** up into **netting** that looked like a spiderweb. "Why don't you pull the red rope, too?" she asked.

"That is the rip cord," said her mother. "It lets the gas out all at once." Carlotta tied her hat **snugly** under her chin. "Sit down!" she ordered. "And hang on!"

Ariel hugged her mother's sturdy legs in their fancy blue gaiters. *Lucky Star* was in the middle of a **misty**, wet, bumpy cloud. The basket went back and forth, up and down, then around and around.

"I feel sick," said Ariel.

"A good aeronaut keeps calm," said Carlotta. "The balloon will cool and we will go down."

She was right. In a few minutes *Lucky Star* was sailing away from the cloud. Carlotta checked everything. "Ropes and toggles are in fine trim," she said. She read the altimeter that hung around her neck. "We are about 2000 feet up." She studied the map and compass. "We are heading south."

"Look!" said Ariel. "The lake is straight ahead."

Just then they saw *Flying Cloud*. "He is beating us," said Ariel. "He will win the gold medal."

Carlotta shook her head. "I have a few tricks yet," she said. "Perhaps we can find a faster stream of air below us." She valved out gas. Down . . . down . . . down went *Lucky Star*. It was sinking too fast—and toward a town! Carlotta tossed handfuls of sand over the side. *Lucky Star* moved up and **skimmed** the rooftops. People stopped whatever they were doing and stared at the balloon.

Suddenly wind stung Ariel's cheeks. "Heigh-ho!" cried Carlotta. "We found the airstream!"

Stop here for the Strategy Break.

Strategy Break

What has happened in Part 2 so far? In the space below—and on another sheet of paper if necessary—write a brief summary. Be sure to include only the most important elements of the story.

_____

_____

_____

_____

_____

_____

Go on reading to see what happens.

It was Ariel who first saw a spiky church steeple coming toward them. "Look out!" she yelled. She closed her eyes and hung on. Carlotta threw out more sand. Just in time! *Lucky Star* **soared** over the steeple.

Now *Flying Cloud* was behind. "If we don't hit another updraft," said Carlotta, "we might win."

Soon they were sweeping over the lake. "There is only a little sand left," Carlotta said. "Let's hope the wind blows us right across."

The air was cold. *Lucky Star*'s gas cooled. They went down. Carlotta tossed out the last handful of sand. But it was not enough.

"Oh, thumps!" cried Ariel. "We'll crash into the lake!"

"Let's keep our wits about us," said Carlotta, "and make the basket lighter."

Ariel helped throw out a raincoat, rubber boots, the Odds and Ends box, and the anchor. Everything went over the side except Harry and his cage.

Lucky Star wobbled and took a giant step. "Lean on this side," said Carlotta. The basket creaked and tilted toward shore.

Lucky Star was almost there, when SPLAAAAASH! The basket plunked into the water. But it didn't sink. The balloon kept it **afloat**.

"We lost the race," cried Ariel, "and it is all my fault. I am extra weight." Ariel knew what she had to do. She held her nose and jumped into the lake. The water was only up to her waist.

"Good gracious!" said her mother. "That was brave, but it will not help. Even without you, the basket is too wet and heavy to go up again."

Just then *Flying Cloud* began to come down. "Our last chance!" cried Carlotta. She threw the guide rope to Ariel. "Pull! Pull us to shore! Hurry!"

Ariel grabbed the rope and waded onto the beach. *Lucky Star* was easy to pull with a balloon holding it up. "Splendid!" cried Carlotta. She jumped out and dragged the basket to higher ground. A minute later *Flying Cloud* landed.

"We won! We won!" shouted Ariel and Carlotta. They were laughing and hugging and crying all at the same time.

Bernard the Brave anchored his balloon to a tree. Then he came over and shook Carlotta's hand. "Congratulations!" he said. "I see that *Lucky Star* has a crew." He wrapped Ariel in a blanket.

"Thank you, sir," said Ariel.

Bernard smiled. "Why, it is my pleasure."

Carlotta sent Harry home with a **victory** message to Balloon Farm. Soon the crowd arrived. Mr. Myers rode up in the buggy. Carlotta told him how Ariel had helped win the race.

"Ariel," he said, "I'm proud of you."

The mayor gave Ariel the gold medal.

Carlotta hugged Ariel. "I'm proud of you, too," she said. "Perhaps you *are* old enough to fly."

Ariel smiled happily. She was sure of it. ●

Strategy Follow-up

Copy the following story map onto a sheet of paper. Fill in Events 7–12 and the Solution. Then, on the same sheet of paper, summarize the end of the story. Use your story map to help you write your summary.

Problem: Ariel wants to go up in the balloon, but her mother tells her she's too young.

▼

Events:

▼

Solution:

✓Personal Checklist

Read each question and put a check (✓) in the correct box.

1. How well were you able to predict what would happen in Part 2 of *The Big Balloon Race*?
   ☐ 3   (extremely well)
   ☐ 2   (fairly well)
   ☐ 1   (not well)

2. How well do you understand what happens in Parts 1 and 2 of this story?
   ☐ 3   (extremely well)
   ☐ 2   (fairly well)
   ☐ 1   (not well)

3. How well do you understand why Ariel's parents are proud of her?
   ☐ 3   (extremely well)
   ☐ 2   (fairly well)
   ☐ 1   (not well)

4. In the Vocabulary Builder, how many words were you able to define by using their root words and context clues?
   ☐ 3   (6–8 words)
   ☐ 2   (3–5 words)
   ☐ 1   (0–2 words)

5. In the Strategy Follow-up, how well were you able to use your story map to write your summary?
   ☐ 3   (extremely well)
   ☐ 2   (fairly well)
   ☐ 1   (not well)

Vocabulary Check

Look back at the work you did in the Vocabulary Builder. Then answer each question by circling the correct letter.

1. What is the root word of *stared*?
   a. stare
   b. star
   c. stay

2. Which vocabulary word would you be able to figure out by using the context clue "wet"?
   a. netting
   b. snugly
   c. misty

3. What does the root word of *victory* mean?
   a. balloonist
   b. loser
   c. winner

4. In the story, *Lucky Star* skimmed the rooftops. What does *skimmed* mean?
   a. moved lightly over
   b. landed upon
   c. flew high above

5. Which vocabulary word means "floating in the air"?
   a. soared
   b. afloat
   c. skimmed

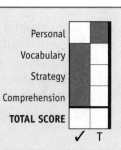

Add the numbers that you just checked to get your Personal Checklist score. Fill in your score here. Then turn to page 201 and transfer your score onto Graph 1.

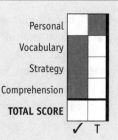

Check your answers with your teacher. Give yourself 1 point for each correct answer, and fill in your Vocabulary score here. Then turn to page 201 and transfer your score onto Graph 1.

Strategy Check

Review your summaries and story map. Then answer these questions:

1. Which sentence describes Event 7 on your story map?
   a. Ariel jumps out of the balloon.
   b. Ariel and her mother get caught in a rain cloud.
   c. Ariel and Carlotta pull the balloon to shore.

2. Which sentence describes Event 12 on your story map?
   a. Carlotta finds an airstream, and they pull ahead of *Flying Cloud.*
   b. Ariel and her mother get caught in a rain cloud.
   c. Ariel and Carlotta pull the balloon to shore.

3. Which of the following does *not* belong in a summary of Part 2?
   a. Carlotta sends Harry to Balloon Farm with a victory message.
   b. Ariel gets sick when she and Carlotta get caught in a rain cloud.
   c. Ariel falls asleep in *Lucky Star* during the mayor's long speech.

4. Which sentence summarizes this entire story?
   a. Ariel and her mother win the big balloon race.
   b. Ariel and her mother don't finish the big balloon race.
   c. Ariel makes her mother lose the big balloon race.

5. What is the solution to this story's problem?
   a. Carlotta says that perhaps Ariel is old enough to fly.
   b. Bernard the Brave lands *Flying Cloud.*
   c. Mr. Myers arrives in his buggy.

Comprehension Check

Review the story if necessary. Then answer these questions:

1. How do Carlotta and Ariel get away from the raincloud?
   a. The balloon cools and goes down.
   b. The balloon cools and goes up.
   c. The balloon heats and goes down.

2. How does *Lucky Star* move ahead of *Flying Cloud*?
   a. Ariel jumps out of *Lucky Star.*
   b. Carlotta finds a faster stream of air.
   c. They throw things out of *Lucky Star.*

3. What happens when Carlotta tosses out handfuls of sand?
   a. The balloon drops down.
   b. The balloon rises up.
   c. The balloon stays in the same place.

4. What character trait does Ariel show when she jumps into the lake?
   a. anger
   b. fear
   c. bravery

5. At the end of the story, why does Carlotta tell Ariel, "Perhaps you *are* old enough to fly"?
   a. because Ariel helped her win the race
   b. because Ariel is ten years old
   c. because Ariel is strong enough to pull a balloon

Check your answers with your teacher. Give yourself 1 point for each correct answer, and fill in your Strategy score here. Then turn to page 201 and transfer your score onto Graph 1.

Personal
Vocabulary
Strategy
Comprehension
TOTAL SCORE
✓ T

Check your answers with your teacher. Give yourself 1 point for each correct answer, and fill in your Comprehension score here. Then turn to page 201 and transfer your score onto Graph 1.

Personal
Vocabulary
Strategy
Comprehension
TOTAL SCORE
✓ T

Extending

Choose one or both of these activities:

PERFORM READER'S THEATER

Get together with a small group of classmates to put on a reader's theater performance of one or both parts of *The Big Balloon Race*. First, assign roles. There are five acting parts: Carlotta, Ariel, Mr. Myers, Bernard, and the mayor. One student should also be the narrator and should read the descriptions in the story. Then practice your lines. After you have rehearsed a few times, perform the selection for your class.

WRITE ABOUT THE MYERS FAMILY

Do some research on the Myers family. Then use some of the information you find to write either a report or another historical-fiction story about them. You might write about life on Balloon Farm. Or you might write about a different balloon race that Carlotta and Ariel take part in.

Resources

Books

Denman, Cherry. *Make Your Own Adventure Story.* Little Brown, 1999.

Roddy, Ruth Mae. *Monologues for Kids.* Dramaline Publications, 1992.

Web Site

http://www.aibf.org
This site from the Albuquerque International Balloon Festival has many photos of colorful, decorative hot-air balloons.

LESSON 12 Hot Air Ballooning

Building Background

Maybe you've never flown in a hot air balloon, but you've probably seen a picture of one. And if you read *The Big Balloon Race* in Lessons 10 and 11, you probably have some idea of how hot air balloons work. In the chart below, fill in the first column with at least three things that you know about hot air balloons. In the second column, write three questions about hot air ballooning that you would like the selection to answer. Leave the third column blank for now. You will fill it in after you have finished reading this selection.

Hot Air Balloons

K (What I **K**now)	W (What I **W**ant to Know)	L (What I **L**earned)
1.	1.	1.
2.	2.	2.
3.	3.	3.

ballast

currents

expands

flutter

inflate

launch

molecules

steer

Vocabulary Builder

1. The words in the margin are specialized vocabulary words. As you learned in Lesson 5, **specialized vocabulary** words are all related to a particular topic in some way. For example, in "Bridges," the words *anchorages, arch, deck,* and *piers* all describe parts of a bridge.

2. Read the words and phrases below. Draw a line from each word in Column 1 to its definition in Column 2. (Use a dictionary if you need help.) Then think about how each word might be used in a selection about hot air balloons.

3. Save your work. You will use it again in the Vocabulary Check.

Column 1	Column 2
ballast	spreads out or gets bigger
currents	streams of air
expands	particles of matter
flutter	drive or direct
inflated	send off or set in motion
launch	extra weight
molecules	blown up
steer	wave or shake

Strategy Builder

Following the Steps in a Process

- When writers describe the process of how something works or is made, they describe the steps in **sequence**. To make the sequence as clear as possible, writers often use **signal words**. Pay attention to the sequence in the following paragraph:

> Paul needed to wash and dry his hair in a hurry. <u>First</u>, he stuck his head under the faucet and got his hair all wet. <u>Next</u>, he poured some shampoo into his hand. <u>Then</u> he rubbed it into his hair. <u>After a few minutes</u> he had worked up a good lather. So he <u>finally</u> rinsed the shampoo out. <u>Last</u>, he used a blow dryer to dry his hair.

- If you wanted to track the sequence of events in the paragraph above, you could put them on a **sequence chain**. It might look like this:

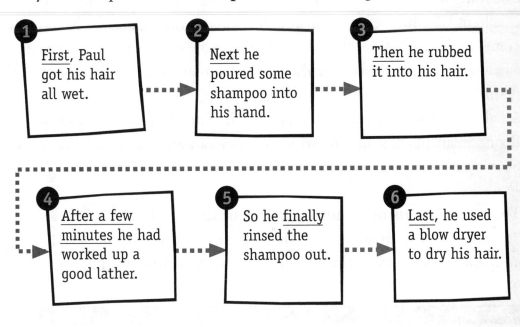

Hot Air Ballooning

by Christie Costanzo

As you read the first part of this selection, you can apply the strategies that you just learned. Notice the signal words. They will give you a more exact picture of the sequence of events.

How Does a Hot Air Balloon Work?

Have you ever wondered what makes a balloon rise up into the air? And once it goes up, how it gets back down? When air is heated, it **expands**. This creates more space between the **molecules**, making the air lighter. Hot air is lighter than cold air. When a balloon is filled with hot air, it rises. When the air inside of the balloon begins to cool, the balloon starts to drop.

Gas-filled balloons are different. They use special gases which are lighter than air. Hydrogen and helium are the two most common gases used for ballooning. The gas-filled balloon can be brought down to earth by letting some of the gas escape.

Imagine that a balloon is sailing above the trees and the wind suddenly changes. The balloon is heading for a mountain. How can the pilot make the balloon climb higher into the sky so that it won't hit the mountain?

If the pilot is in a gas-filled balloon, the balloonist must throw something overboard. Balloonists in gas balloons carry extra weight called **ballast**. The ballast is thrown out to make the balloon lighter. Once the ballast is thrown out, the balloon can climb higher.

If the pilot is in a hot-air balloon, the balloonist can shoot a flame into the opening of the balloon with the burner. This will heat up the air inside the balloon. The hotter the air inside the balloon, the lighter the balloon becomes and the higher it flies. The pilot must be careful not to overheat the balloon. This could damage the fabric and make holes at the top of the balloon.

A balloon must go where the wind takes it. The pilot cannot **steer** the balloon. Smart pilots study the weather. They can tell which way the wind is blowing by watching the leaves **fluttering** on a tree or a flag waving on a pole.

There are **currents** of air flowing above the earth. When the pilot wants to fly to the east, he or she tries to find a river of air moving in that direction. Sometimes the wind closer to the ground is blowing to the east, while the wind a thousand feet above the ground is blowing to the west. Under these conditions, a clever pilot could **launch** and land the balloon from the same area. The pilot would fly to the east in the lower current and then come back in the upper current. This does not happen very often.

Preparing the Balloon for Liftoff

Most balloon flights occur in the early morning when the air is cool and calm. A pilot will not launch a balloon if it is raining or if the wind is too strong. A light breeze, under 10 mph, and clear skies are the best flying conditions.

The launch area is selected with safety in mind. The site should be well away from tall trees and high powerlines. There should be plenty of room to lay out the fabric bag on a smooth surface. The ground crew checks for rocks and other sharp objects which might tear a hole in the balloon. Once the area is clear, the balloon can be rolled out.

There are special numbers marked on the balloon fabric. These numbers help the crew lay out the balloon properly. In this way they can keep the balloon's ropes from becoming twisted and tangled.

The fuel tanks are loaded into the wicker basket. The basket is tipped on its side while the burner is mounted on its bracket. Next the cables and ropes, which hold the balloon to the basket, are attached.

Stop here for the Strategy Break.

Strategy Break

If you were to arrange the steps in "Preparing the Balloon for Liftoff," so far, your sequence chain might look like this:

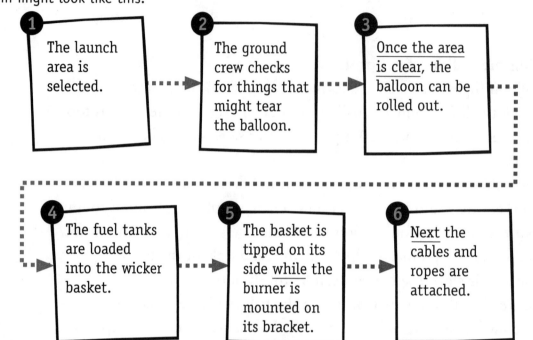

As you continue reading, keep track of the rest of the steps in "Preparing the Balloon for Liftoff." Also keep looking for signal words. You will use them later to create a sequence chain of your own.

Go on reading.

Now the balloon is ready to be **inflated**. It takes two steps to inflate the balloon. First, the balloon is filled with cold air and then the air is heated. The crew members go to their positions. One person must hold the crown line. This is the rope attached to the top of the balloon. The person holding the crown line will keep the balloon from "standing up" too soon.

Two more people are needed to hold ropes on either side of the balloon. These ropes help spread out the balloon while it is being inflated. If it is windy more people will be needed to hold the balloon in place.

Once all the lines are secured, the cold inflation can begin. A huge gasoline-powered fan is wheeled near the mouth of the balloon. With arms stretched overhead, the pilot or crew member holds the balloon open for inflation. The fan is started. Soon a steady stream of air is pushed into the mouth of the balloon.

The fabric flutters and stirs. Within minutes the balloon begins to take shape. It looks like a giant whale sleeping on the beach. Stepping inside the balloon, the pilot checks the fabric for holes or tears. The pilot also tests the rip panel at the crown of the balloon and the maneuvering vent. Before leaving the balloon, the pilot gathers up the ripcord, the vent cord, and the pyrometer cord and carries them outside. Then the pilot attaches each one to its proper place on the basket.

The air bag is almost two-thirds full. It is time to use the burner. The end of the burner is aimed at the middle of the balloon's opening. Long hot blasts are used to warm the air inside the balloon. As the air warms up and expands, the balloon grows larger and larger. The crew must hold the ropes very tight. If the balloon is allowed to "stand up" too soon, it could roll over or twist to the side.

The pilot continues to shoot hot flames into the balloon. As the balloon fills out, the pilot orders the crew to "ease off" on their lines. Without letting go completely, the crew members relax their grip. Soon the balloon will be ready to rise off the ground. After a few more blasts from the burner, the pilot shouts, "Let her up!" Everyone drops their ropes at once and the big colorful balloon pops up into position. The crew cheers. Their balloon is standing.

The basket is now seated correctly on its base. The pilot is in the basket in case the balloon should fly away. The balloon is kept in place by the crew. They lean on the edge of the basket with two hands. The pilot checks the instruments. Everything seems to be working. The pilot is ready for his passengers to climb aboard. The passengers are helped into the basket.

The rest of the ground crew has loaded the big fan and extra tanks of fuel into the chase vehicle. Everyone is ready to go.

The pilot turns the valve of the burner and the bluish flames shoot up. The balloon wants to fly. The people holding the basket have to press down with all their weight to keep the balloon on the ground.

"Hands off," calls the pilot and immediately the balloon takes to the sky. "Good-bye," wave the ground crew before piling into the chase vehicle.

"Good-bye," wave the passengers as they float higher and higher into the morning sky. A slight breeze begins to push them gently to the east. ●

Strategy Follow-up

First, go back and fill in the third column of the K-W-L chart on page 114. Then list the rest of the steps in the process of preparing the balloon for liftoff. Begin with Step 7. Underline any signal words that you use.

7 The balloon is inflated:
1. First,

2. Then

8 As the balloon fills out,

9 After a few more blasts

10 The balloon is standing, and the basket

11 The passengers

12

✓Personal Checklist

Read each question and put a check (✓) in the correct box.

1. How well would you be able to tell someone else what makes a balloon rise and drop?
   - ☐ 3 (extremely well)
   - ☐ 2 (fairly well)
   - ☐ 1 (not well)

2. How well do you understand the process of preparing a balloon for liftoff?
   - ☐ 3 (extremely well)
   - ☐ 2 (fairly well)
   - ☐ 1 (not well)

3. On the K-W-L chart, how well were you able to list three things that you learned from reading this selection?
   - ☐ 3 (extremely well)
   - ☐ 2 (fairly well)
   - ☐ 1 (not well)

4. In the Vocabulary Builder, how well were you able to match the specialized vocabulary words and their definitions?
   - ☐ 3 (extremely well)
   - ☐ 2 (fairly well)
   - ☐ 1 (not well)

5. How well were you able to complete the sequence chain in the Strategy Follow-up?
   - ☐ 3 (extremely well)
   - ☐ 2 (fairly well)
   - ☐ 1 (not well)

Vocabulary Check

Look back at the work you did in the Vocabulary Builder. Then answer each question by circling the correct letter.

1. What does the word *current* mean in the context of this selection?
   - a. up to date
   - b. stream of air
   - c. flow of electricity

2. Which vocabulary word were you able to figure out using the context clue "extra weight"?
   - a. inflate
   - b. ballast
   - c. expands

3. Which of these things flutters in the wind?
   - a. a butterfly's wings
   - b. a stone statue
   - c. both of the above

4. Which of these objects can you inflate?
   - a. a basketball
   - b. a bicycle tire
   - c. both of the above

5. A pilot will not launch a balloon if the wind is too strong. What does *launch* mean?
   - a. land
   - b. send off
   - c. fill with air

Add the numbers that you just checked to get your Personal Checklist score. Fill in your score here. Then turn to page 201 and transfer your score onto Graph 1.

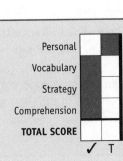

Personal
Vocabulary
Strategy
Comprehension
TOTAL SCORE
✓ T

Check your answers with your teacher. Give yourself 1 point for each correct answer, and fill in your Vocabulary score here. Then turn to page 201 and transfer your score onto Graph 1.

Personal
Vocabulary
Strategy
Comprehension
TOTAL SCORE
✓ T

Strategy Check

Review the sequence chain you that completed in the Strategy Follow-up. Also review the rest of the selection. Then answer these questions:

1. What is the first step in inflating the balloon?
   a. The balloon is filled with cold air.
   b. The air in the balloon is heated.
   c. The pilot steps inside the balloon.

2. When is the basket finally seated on its base?
   a. right after the pilot gets into it
   b. after it's filled with hot air from the burner
   c. after the crew loads the chase vehicle

3. During which step on your sequence chain does the pilot yell, "Hands off"?
   a. Step 3
   b. Step 5
   c. Step 6

4. Which of the following is *not* an example of a signal word or words?
   a. as the balloon fills out
   b. without letting go completely
   c. immediately

5. Which signal word could you use to introduce the last step in a process?
   a. first
   b. then
   c. finally

Comprehension Check

Review the selection if necessary. Then answer these questions:

1. How does the pilot in a gas-filled balloon make the balloon climb higher?
   a. The pilot shoots a flame into the balloon.
   b. The pilot lets out some of the gas.
   c. The pilot throws ballast overboard.

2. Why do balloon pilots watch the leaves fluttering on a tree?
   a. to find out which way the wind is blowing
   b. to launch and land a balloon from the same area
   c. to heat the air inside a balloon

3. Why do you think the balloon's launch area should be well away from tall trees?
   a. so everyone can clearly see the balloon sail away
   b. so the pilot can study the weather
   c. so the balloon doesn't get tangled in the branches

4. What could happen if a balloon is allowed to pop up too soon?
   a. It could fly away.
   b. It could roll or twist.
   c. It could tear.

5. What do you think is the purpose of the chase vehicle?
   a. to follow and help the balloonist if needed
   b. to create wind so the balloon will rise higher
   c. to let the pilot know where to find strong air currents

Check your answers with your teacher. Give yourself 1 point for each correct answer, and fill in your Strategy score here. Then turn to page 201 and transfer your score onto Graph 1.

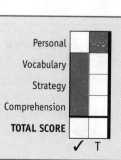

Check your answers with your teacher. Give yourself 1 point for each correct answer, and fill in your Comprehension score here. Then turn to page 201 and transfer your score onto Graph 1.

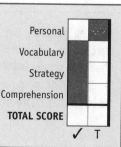

Extending

Choose one or both of these activities:

DO A SCIENCE EXPERIMENT

You can perform an experiment to see how hot and cold air affect a balloon. First get two empty soda or water bottles. Place a normal-sized balloon over the mouth of each of bottle. Place each bottle in a deep pan. Fill one pan with hot water. Fill the other pan with ice water. What happens to the two balloons? Write down the results and share them with your class. Or, if you can, carry out the experiment in class. For ideas on other experiments that you can do with balloons, check out the resources listed on this page.

MAKE YOUR OWN BALLOON

Draw, paint, or sculpt your own hot air balloon. Include any of your favorite symbols, numbers, or colors. Be sure to include the balloon's basket, cables, and ropes.

Resources

Books

Ames, Lee J. *Draw 50 Airplanes, Aircraft and Spacecraft.* Bt Bound, 1999.

Kaner, Etta. *Balloon Science.* Perseus Press, 1990.

Pearce, Q. L. *60 Super Simple Science Experiements.* Lowell House, 1998.

Web Site

http://www.launch.net/index.shtml
This site has news and information about the sport of ballooning.

Building Background

Think about a time when you did something all by yourself. Maybe you finished a difficult homework assignment on your own. Or maybe you made something without anyone else's help. How did you feel when you finished? On the lines below, describe what you did and how you felt about it. Then keep those feelings in mind as you begin reading "Derby."

_____

_____

_____

_____

_____

_____

_____

_____

announcer

championship

compete

disqualified

exterior

gleefully

hooted

nudged

outstretched

Vocabulary Builder

1. The boldfaced words in the questions below are all from the story "Derby." Before you read the story, answer the questions with a partner.

2. If you can't figure out any of the words, find them in the story, read them in context, and then try to figure them out. Then go back and answer the questions. See how many you can answer without using a dictionary.

3. Save your work. You will use it again in the Vocabulary Check.

   a. Is the **exterior** of something its outside, inside, or middle?

   _____

   b. When you say something **gleefully**, are you sad, happy, or scared?

   _____

c. If someone **nudged** you, would you be bumped very hard or very softly?

_____

d. Do the people who **compete** in a game watch it, judge it, or take part in it?

_____

e. Who would you expect to get the **championship** trophy—the loser or the winner of a game?

_____

f. If you are **disqualified** from a sport, are you allowed to play or not?

_____

g. Are **outstretched** arms held apart, crossed, or together?

_____

h. Would you expect an **announcer** to tell what's happening at a sporting event or sit and watch the event?

_____

i. If someone in an audience **hooted,** would it be very soft, very loud, or not heard at all?

_____

Strategy Builder

Making Predictions While Reading a Story

- When you read, you often make predictions. As you know, a **prediction** is a kind of guess. When you make predictions, you base them on clues from the story. For example, you can base your predictions on events that have already happened in the story. Or you can base them on what you know about the characters.

- In "Derby" there are two main characters—Quincy Jacobs and his father Grady. As you read this story, notice what Quincy and Grady say and do. You might be able to base your predictions on some of their words and actions.

Derby

by Michael O. Tunnell

As you read this story, look for clues that will help you predict what might happen next. In particular, notice what the characters say and do.

"I got it!" Quincy yelled as he battered open the front door. He waved a small blue-and-yellow box above his head.

His dad, covered with flour, rushed from the kitchen. Quincy stuffed the box into his **outstretched** hands.

"Your first Pinewood Derby kit," Grady Jacobs said proudly. "Come on, let's look."

They opened the box, and a rectangular block of wood, four plastic wheels, and some shiny nails slid onto the kitchen counter.

"But it doesn't look like a car at all," said Quincy.

"Ah, Quinn, the car is inside the block. We cut it and carve it and sand it until we have the fastest, sharpest derby car in your Cub Scout pack. I built them every year when I was a scout. Won twice, you know."

Quincy smiled. "Yes, I know."

That evening Quincy and his dad went down to the basement workshop, a corner with a teetering workbench and tools hanging on pegboards. "Now, Quinn," Grady said seriously, "the car cannot be longer than seven inches or wider than two and three-fourths inches. And it can't weigh more than five ounces. It will be faster, however, if it weighs exactly five ounces and is streamlined like a sports car."

Grady reached for a pencil, marked a slanted line on the block of wood, and used a vise to hold it in place while he cut a sleek wedge shape. Quincy watched.

Grady used a jigsaw to scoop out a fin on the back of the car. Quincy watched.

Grady rubbed the car with sandpaper until it was smooth and nicely rounded. Quincy watched.

"It's getting late," said Grady. "I'll let you sand the flat surfaces tomorrow. We did good work, son."

The next day Quincy raced home from school and thumped down the basement stairs, only to find his dad about to drill holes in the bottom of the derby car.

"I got home early, so I sanded the top and sides. And I weighed the car on our postal scale. Look here."

Grady laid the wooden wedge on the scale, along with the wheels and the nails that would serve as axles. "See, the whole thing only weighs a little more than three ounces. So, I'll drill a hole in the bottom and put in these fishing weights." He added several lead weights to the scale until it showed nearly five ounces.

"Can I use the drill, Dad?" asked Quincy.

"Well, this is a tricky job. It's hard not to drill right through the car. Just watch for now," said Grady as he secured the wedge of wood with a clamp.

So Quincy watched the drilling. He watched his dad drop the fishing weights into the hollow and cover them with wood putty. Quincy wanted to glop on the putty, but Grady said it was hard to get smooth.

Quincy gazed at the Pinewood Derby racer, remembering how long it had taken to get his hands on the electric train his dad had given him for Christmas. Grady loved trains, too.

⬢ Stop here for Strategy Break #1.

Strategy Break #1

1. What do you predict will happen next?_____

_____

_____

2. Why do you think so?_____

_____

_____

3. What clues from the story helped you make your prediction(s)?_____

_____

_____

 Go on reading to see what happens.

By the time Quincy got home the next afternoon, Grady was blowing dust from the freshly sanded car.

"Just in time to watch me paint," Grady said, rubbing his hands together **gleefully**. "It isn't easy. You have to put on several light coats so the paint won't drip or run."

Quincy watched his dad apply the first coat of red spray paint.

Over the next few days, Quincy watched his dad add another coat of paint, sand with fine sandpaper, and paint again. He also watched as Grady slipped the shiny nails through the wheels and into slots carved in the bottom of the racer. He watched as Grady sanded the wheels smooth and used black powder, called graphite, to lubricate the nails so the wheels would turn faster.

Finally, Grady painted yellow streaks of lightning on the cherry red racer. Then he asked Quincy what number the car should have. Quincy smiled and shrugged, so Grady chose number seven. "For good luck," he said.

The night of the race, the school gym was teeming with people. After Quincy's mom found a place to sit, Quincy and his dad made their way to the Pit, where kids could make last-minute adjustments before their cars were weighed and registered.

"We've got a car to register," Grady told the official-looking man standing behind an official-looking scale. "A fast car." The man weighed the cherry red racer—five ounces on the nose.

"Well, everybody," Grady said as they returned to the bleachers, "prepare for victory!"

A big man in a scout uniform called for attention. "Gentlemen, start your engines," he cried. The crowd laughed, and the races began.

People jumped up and down, cheering and yelling, as red and yellow and green and purple cars plunged down the long, steep track. The cherry red racer with yellow lightning bolts never lost a single race. Grady jumped and yelled and **hooted** with each victory.

Another car kept winning, too. It was thick and rounded, as if only the points had been sanded off each corner of the wooden block. But what made it really stand out, besides winning, was its shiny **exterior**. The whole car was covered with thumbtacks, blue paint peeking out in between.

"Looks like that's the car to beat," said Grady nervously. "I'd never have thought of using thumbtacks for weight. Do you know the owner? Jacob Brady? And where'd he come up with a number like 75–85?"

Quincy smiled and shook his head.

Both cars continued to win until the "Thumbtack Special" and the cherry red racer were left to **compete** against one another for the **championship**. The champion would have to win two out of three races. As the two racers were placed on the starting line, the crowd seemed to stop breathing. But as the starter dropped the bar and released the cars, bodies leaped up from the bleachers.

"Go number seven!"

"Go! Go! Go! Number 75–85!"

"Faster, faster, Yellow Lightning!"

"Hurry, 'Tackmobile!"

The cherry red racer **nudged** across the finish line just ahead of the Thumbtack Special. Grady leaped into the air and screeched with delight. Quincy smiled.

Again the cars were released onto the track. Down they rushed, rattling in their grooves. This time the Thumbtack Special crossed the line first. Grady slapped his forehead and groaned. Quincy smiled.

"The winner of the next race will be the champion," barked the **announcer**, as the cherry red racer and the Thumbtack Special were lined up one last time.

When the starting bar was dropped, the crowd roared to its feet. Neck and neck the two cars flashed down the track. But just before the finish line, the cherry red racer pulled ahead. Grady jumped up and down in a wild victory dance.

The announcer cleared his throat, signaling for attention. "Would the Cubs with the winning cars come forward as I call their names? The award for the fastest Cub Scout Pinewood Derby racer goes to Quincy Jacobs!" The crowd whooped and halloed, and Grady nudged Quincy forward to accept the small golden trophy.

"The second-fastest car belongs to . . ." Suddenly Quincy's den mother was standing next to the announcer, whispering in his ear. A shocked expression washed over the announcer's face, but then he smiled and nodded.

⬣ **Stop here for Strategy Break #2.**

Strategy Break #2

1. Do your earlier predictions match what happened? _____ Why or why not? _____
   _____

2. What do you predict will happen next?_____
   _____

3. Why do you think so?_____
   _____

4. What clues from the story helped you make your prediction(s)?_____
   _____

➡️ **Go on reading to see what happens.**

"The second-fastest car belongs to . . . Quincy Jacobs!" The announcer laughed and held aloft the Thumbtack Special.

"Now, before any of you get upset," the announcer continued, "Quincy's second car is **disqualified**. He and Mrs. Blumberg, Quincy's den mother, entered it under an assumed name, not thinking it would do so well. Quincy built the car secretly, all by himself. Anyway, Mrs. Blumberg apologizes and—"

"Wait!"

The crowd turned as Grady stood up.

"Ah, I'm Quincy's dad and I think the red racer is the one to be disqualified. I know Pinewood Derby is a father-and-son project, but there's too much father in that red car. Quincy built the other one by himself. It should win."

The crowd and the announcer were silent, and then a great cheer rose from the bleachers.

On the way home, Quincy sat in the front seat with his dad.

"Your Thumbtack Special was really something," Grady said.

"I worked on it at night, when all of you were upstairs. It took nearly a whole box of thumbtacks."

"The number was a great idea, Quincy," said his mom, leaning forward from the backseat.

"What? Did I miss something?" Grady picked the Thumbtack Special off Quincy's lap and squinted at the number. "Oh, very good, Quinn. Your birth date! Seventh month, fifth day of 1985: 7–5–85. The July 5th Special!"

Quincy laughed.

"Banana splits when we get home," announced Grady. "And afterward, we'll move Quincy's electric train out of my office into his bedroom!" ●

Strategy Follow-up

Go back and look at the predictions that you wrote in this lesson. Do any of them match what actually happened in this story? Why or why not? _____

_____

_____

_____

_____

✓Personal Checklist

Read each question and put a check (✓) in the correct box.

1. How well do you understand what happened in "Derby"?
   - ☐ 3 (extremely well)
   - ☐ 2 (fairly well)
   - ☐ 1 (not well)

2. How well do you understand why Grady asked the announcer to disqualify the red racer?
   - ☐ 3 (extremely well)
   - ☐ 2 (fairly well)
   - ☐ 1 (not well)

3. In Building Background, how well did what you wrote help you understand why Quincy built his Thumbtack Special?
   - ☐ 3 (extremely well)
   - ☐ 2 (fairly well)
   - ☐ 1 (not well)

4. In the Vocabulary Builder, how many questions did you answer correctly and without using a dictionary?
   - ☐ 3 (7–9 questions)
   - ☐ 2 (4–6 questions)
   - ☐ 1 (0–3 questions)

5. How well were you able to predict what would happen next in this story?
   - ☐ 3 (extremely well)
   - ☐ 2 (fairly well)
   - ☐ 1 (not well)

Vocabulary Check

Look back at the work you did in the Vocabulary Builder. Then answer each question by circling the correct letter.

1. While Grady builds the red racer, he rubs his hands gleefully. What does *gleefully* mean?
   a. happily
   b. sadly
   c. angrily

2. Quincy stuck thumbtacks all over the exterior of his car. Which part of the car is the exterior?
   a. the inside
   b. the middle
   c. the outside

3. What does the word *hoot* mean in the context of this story?
   a. sound made by a person
   b. sound made by an owl
   c. sound made by a horn

4. Which word best describes the red racer after Grady said the other car should win?
   a. nudged
   b. disqualified
   c. hooted

5. Both Quincy and Grady race cars at the derby. Which word best describes what they do there?
   a. outstretched
   b. disqualified
   c. compete

Add the numbers that you just checked to get your Personal Checklist score. Fill in your score here. Then turn to page 201 and transfer your score onto Graph 1.

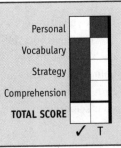

Check your answers with your teacher. Give yourself 1 point for each correct answer, and fill in your Vocabulary score here. Then turn to page 201 and transfer your score onto Graph 1.

Strategy Check

Look back at what you wrote at each Strategy Break. Then answer these questions:

1. At Strategy Break #1, if you had predicted that Grady would not let Quincy help, which clue would have best supported your prediction?

    a. "I'll let you sand the flat surfaces tomorrow."

    b. Quincy watched.

    c. "We did good work, son."

2. Which clue suggests Grady had taken over before?

    a. Grady laid the wooden wedge on the scale, along with the wheels and the nails that would serve as axles.

    b. He added several lead weights to the scale until it showed nearly five ounces.

    c. Quincy remembered how long it had taken to get his hands on the electric train his dad had given him for Christmas.

3. At Strategy Break #2, which prediction would have best fit the story?

    a. The second-fastest car belongs to Quincy.

    b. The second-fastest car belongs to Grady.

    c. The second-fastest car belongs to Mrs. Jacobs.

4. Which clue suggests that Grady was more excited than Quincy was at the derby?

    a. Grady jumped up and down.

    b. Quincy and his dad made their way to the Pit.

    c. Quincy smiled and shook his head.

5. If you had predicted that the second-fastest car belonged to Quincy, which clue would have helped?

    a. the number that he gave it: 75–85

    b. Quincy's smile when Grady asked who Jacob Brady was

    c. the way that Quincy was cheering when the Thumbtack Special won

Comprehension Check

Review the story if necessary. Then answer these questions:

1. Why is Quincy excited when he shows his dad the Pinewood Derby kit?

    a. He wants his dad to build the racer.

    b. He wants to build the racer by himself.

    c. He wants to build the racer with his dad.

2. Why does Quincy secretly build his own racer?

    a. because he doesn't think the red car will win

    b. because his dad won't let him help build the red car

    c. because he wants to beat his dad in the race

3. What does Grady mean when he says "there's too much father in that red car"?

    a. He is proud that he built the car by himself.

    b. The car is old and not very fast.

    c. He should not have built the car without Quincy's help.

4. How did Quincy come up with the number of the Thumbtack Special?

    a. He used the date of his birth.

    b. He picked a lucky number.

    c. He used the date of his father's birth.

5. At the end of the story, why does Grady say that he will move Quincy's train into the boy's bedroom?

    a. Grady doesn't want to play with the train anymore.

    b. Grady knows he's been selfish with Quincy's gift.

    c. Grady is angry and wants to punish Quincy.

Check your answers with your teacher. Give yourself 1 point for each correct answer, and fill in your Strategy score here. Then turn to page 201 and transfer your score onto Graph 1.

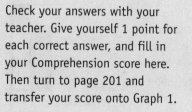

Check your answers with your teacher. Give yourself 1 point for each correct answer, and fill in your Comprehension score here. Then turn to page 201 and transfer your score onto Graph 1.

Extending

Choose one or more of these activities:

HOLD YOUR OWN DERBY

Race small wooden cars in a derby of your own. Paint the cars different colors and write numbers on them. If possible, make the cars all the same weight. When the cars are ready, make your racetrack. Use a shallow cardboard box. You can also use cardboard to make "lanes" in the box. Finally, prop the box so that one end is higher. Hold the cars until everyone is ready, and then let them go at the same time.

RESEARCH THE CUB SCOUTS AND GIRL SCOUTS

The Cub Scouts is an organization for boys ages 8 to 10. The Girl Scouts is an organization for girls over age 8. Find out more about the Cub Scouts and Girl Scouts. Find out what they stand for and what they do for fun. Also find out when, where, and how each organization began. The resources listed on this page can help you get started.

DRAW THE RED RACER OR THE THUMBTACK SPECIAL

Draw a picture of the red racer that Grady built. Or draw Quincy's Thumbtack Special. Or if you'd like, draw both cars speeding down the track during the race.

Resources

Books

Ames, Lee J. *Draw 50 Cars, Trucks and Motorcycles.* Doubleday, 1986.

Boy Scouts of America Staff. *Boy Scouts of America: The Official Handbook for Boys,* reprint of original 1911 edition. Applewood Books, 1997.

Brown, Fern G. *Daisy and the Girl Scouts: The Story of Juliette Gordon Low.* Albert Whitman, 1996.

Web Sites

http://www.girlscouts.org
This is the official Web site of the Girl Scouts of America. It contains almost everything you ever wanted to know about the organization.

http://www.pbs.org/tal/racecars
This Web site lets you build your own online race car.

http://www.scouting.org
This is the official Web site of the Boy Scouts of America. It includes complete information about the organization.

Electric Cars

Building Background

You see cars and buses every day. You probably ride in them fairly often too. Think about the thing that makes cars and buses go—gasoline. Gasoline is an important fuel, but there are some problems with it. For one thing, it is expensive. The price of gasoline is always going up. Another problem with it is the dirty air it causes when it is used in cars and other vehicles.

Some people would like to see gasoline-powered cars replaced by electric cars. But there are problems with using electric cars too. In the selection you are about to read, you will learn about some of those problems. You also will learn the history of electric cars, as well as the progress that researchers have made with them.

exhaust

fuel

pollution

recharged

vehicles

Vocabulary Builder

1. The words in the margin are all in "Electric Cars." Do you know the meanings of these words? If not, making word trees can help you understand them. A word tree can include synonyms, or words that have the same meaning. It also can include examples and a definition of the word. Look at the following word tree for *beautiful:*

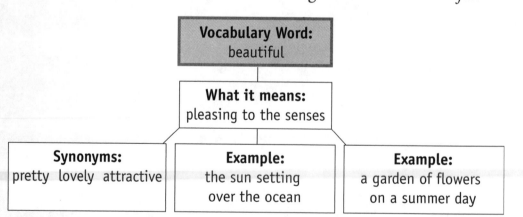

2. On another piece of paper, start a word tree for each vocabulary word. Then, as you read "Electric Cars," fill out each tree with synonyms, examples, and a definition of the word. Use context clues to help you figure out each word's meaning. Or look it up in a dictionary.

3. Save your work. You will use it again in the Vocabulary Check.

Strategy Builder

How to Read an Informational Article

- In Lesson 3 you learned that an **informational article** gives facts and details about a particular **topic**. You also learned that an informational article is organized into **main ideas** and **supporting details**.

- Look through the pages of "Electric Cars." As you can see, the article is divided into several sections. Each section begins with a different heading. The **heading** tells you the main idea of that section. The paragraphs in the section supply details that support the main idea.

- The following paragraph is from an informational article on dinosaurs. The main idea is underlined once. The details that support the main idea are underlined twice.

> ### Dinosaurs' Size
> Dinosaurs were the <u>biggest animals to ever walk the earth</u>. The largest dinosaurs grew to be <u>about 90 feet long</u>. They weighed <u>more than 10 times as much as an elephant</u>. <u>Only a few kinds of whales are larger than the biggest dinosaurs</u>.

- If you wanted to show the main idea and details on a **concept map**, it would look like this:

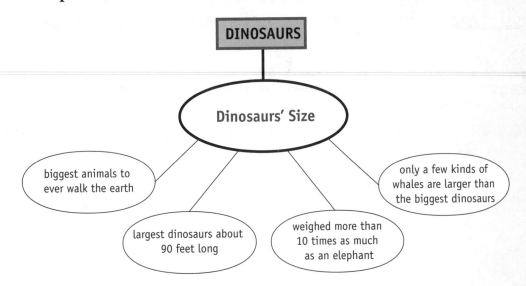

Electric Cars

As you read the beginning of this informational article, you can apply the strategies that you just learned. The main ideas are underlined once. Supporting details are underlined twice.

Try to think of life without cars. It's not easy. But our cars make us sick. Their **exhaust** pollutes the air. Dirty air is hard to breathe. On some days in large cities, the air is thick and gray. Polluted air drifts all over. It even rises high above Earth. Many scientists feel that it can change the weather. Everyone is hurt by **pollution**.

Each day there are more cars, buses, and trucks. Each day they cause more pollution. We can't get rid of our **vehicles**. But we can change them. Their gasoline engines are the problem. Vehicles could be powered some other way. A likely form of energy is electricity. Today, researchers are trying to build a useful electric car.

The electric car is not a new idea. The first electrics were made about 100 years ago. In fact, three kinds of engines were used on early cars.

Early Electrics

Around 1900, thousands of cars ran on electric batteries. They were <u>silent</u>, so they never scared horses. They were <u>clean</u>. They were <u>easy to start</u>. Almost every woman driver chose an electric car.

But electric cars were <u>slow</u>. Their top speed was 20 or 30 miles per hour. Going uphill, top speed fell to 4 or 5 miles per hour. Even worse, they <u>couldn't go far</u>. After about 30 miles, the batteries had to be **recharged**.

 Stop here for the Strategy Break.

Strategy Break

If you were to create a concept map for this article so far, it might look like this:

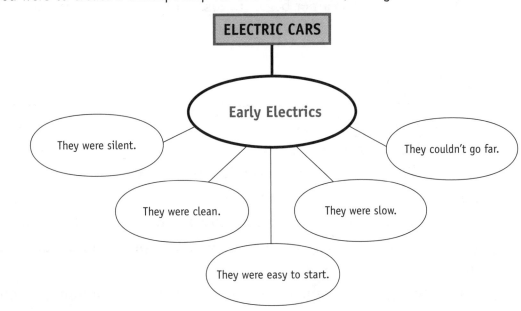

ELECTRIC CARS

Early Electrics

They were silent.

They couldn't go far.

They were clean.

They were slow.

They were easy to start.

As you continue reading "Electric Cars," keep looking for the main ideas and supporting details. At the end of this article, you will use some of them to create a concept map of your own.

 Go on reading.

Some Progress

Other cars had steam engines. A steam-powered car was almost as clean as an electric. And it was much faster. Racing steamers reached speeds of over 100 miles per hour. With normal use, steamers ran at 30 miles per hour for more than 150 miles.

Cars with gasoline engines also went fast. And they had a wider range. Refueling took only minutes. As long as a car could get **fuel**, its range had almost no limits.

But these gasoline-powered cars had drawbacks. There were many moving parts that could break. They often did. A driver had to fix many things on, in, and under the car. Driving one of these cars could be dirty. Worst of all, the engine had to be cranked before the car would start. Only a strong person could do that.

Then, in 1912, the self-starter came into use. Now an electric battery, not a crank, would start a gas-powered car. Suddenly, these cars were as easy to start as electrics. They were already as fast as steamers. Both the electric car and the steamer began to lose ground. Within 20 years, no one made them anymore.

Modern Electrics

In the 1960s, attention turned once more to the electric car. What could increase its speed and range?

Some researchers looked at the lead-acid battery. They tried new designs. They tried different materials. Some batteries they made were better than those of today. But the strongest ones cost too much.

Other researchers worked on a slightly different power source. It is called a fuel cell. A fuel cell could be twice as strong as a lead-acid battery. But, even today, it is too heavy and costly.

Recharging was also studied. Drivers wouldn't mind stopping so often for a recharging if it took only minutes. Still another idea was to design a lighter car. Then a regular battery could push it faster and farther.

Today, many designs are being tested. Large and small companies and even people on their own are building electrics. Reports say that work is moving ahead.

Road Tests

One owner tried to drive cross-country in his modern electric car in 1991. Noel Perrin later wrote about his trip in *Solo: Life with an Electric Car.* Perrin was happy with his car's speed on flat land. The car could go 50 miles per hour easily. It went up to 60 miles between charges. For short bursts, the car could even reach 60 miles per hour.

But going up a steep hill, the car could barely reach 30 miles per hour. Worse, it ran out of power very quickly.

Each time Perrin stopped to recharge, he had big problems. There were no charging stations along the highways. So Perrin had to plug his car into regular outlets. At best, recharging took four hours. Sometimes it took twice that time. That meant that Perrin could travel only about 100 miles a day.

The same year, someone else drove an electric car for 24 hours straight under special conditions. Recharging was much quicker. This car went more than 600 miles.

In 1992, an electric vehicle did even better with a new charging station. A small electric truck was driven around a race track. Every 60 miles or so, it pulled into the station. A computer controlled the recharging. Each time, the job took less than 20 minutes. The truck traveled 831.8 miles in 24 hours, a new world record.

Planning Ahead

Could we have fast charging stations—or electricity pumps—along the roads? These would give electric cars the range they need. But such pumps would cause new problems.

Electric power companies have more than enough energy at night. Electric cars that are recharged at night could use that energy. But suppose that they needed to recharge during the day. Then they would need to stop at electricity pumps. The power companies would have to put out more energy. So the power companies would do more polluting, since coal is used to make electricity. That wouldn't help.

In short, there is little chance that your next car will be an electric. But each step takes researchers a little further. Why not plan ahead? It may be time to start an electric car savings fund. ●

Strategy Follow-up

Now create a concept map for the section of this article called "Modern Electrics." Fill in the topic and main idea of your map. Then fill in details that support the main idea.

✓Personal Checklist

Read each question and put a check (✓) in the correct box.

1. How well do you understand the information given in "Electric Cars"?
   - ☐ 3 (extremely well)
   - ☐ 2 (fairly well)
   - ☐ 1 (not well)

2. How well do you understand why electric cars have not replaced gas-powered cars?
   - ☐ 3 (extremely well)
   - ☐ 2 (fairly well)
   - ☐ 1 (not well)

3. How well did the information in Building Background help you understand why some people want to build electric cars?
   - ☐ 3 (extremely well)
   - ☐ 2 (fairly well)
   - ☐ 1 (not well)

4. In the Vocabulary Builder, how many word trees were you able to complete?
   - ☐ 3 (4–5 word trees)
   - ☐ 2 (2–3 word trees)
   - ☐ 1 (0–1 word trees)

5. In the Strategy Follow-up, how well were you able to list the main idea and supporting details on your concept map?
   - ☐ 3 (extremely well)
   - ☐ 2 (fairly well)
   - ☐ 1 (not well)

Vocabulary Check

Look back at the work you did in the Vocabulary Builder. Then answer each question by circling the correct letter.

1. What could you list on a word tree as an example of *pollution*?
   a. electric cars
   b. car exhaust
   c. electricity

2. Gasoline is an example of which vocabulary word?
   a. fuel
   b. vehicles
   c. exhaust

3. What could you list on a word tree as a definition of *recharge*?
   a. speed up
   b. slow down
   c. fill up

4. *Fumes* is a synonym of which vocabulary word?
   a. fuel
   b. exhaust
   c. recharge

5. For which word could you list *trucks* as an example?
   a. pollution
   b. exhaust
   c. vehicles

Add the numbers that you just checked to get your Personal Checklist score. Fill in your score here. Then turn to page 201 and transfer your score onto Graph 1.

Personal
Vocabulary
Strategy
Comprehension
TOTAL SCORE
✓ T

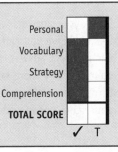

Check your answers with your teacher. Give yourself 1 point for each correct answer, and fill in your Vocabulary score here. Then turn to page 201 and transfer your score onto Graph 1.

Personal
Vocabulary
Strategy
Comprehension
TOTAL SCORE
✓ T

Strategy Check

Review the concept map that you created in the Strategy Follow-up. Also review the rest of the article. Then answer these questions:

1. What did you list as the main idea on your concept map?
   a. Early Electrics
   b. Modern Electrics
   c. Road Tests

2. Which of the following would *not* appear as a supporting detail on your concept map?
   a. Other researchers worked on a fuel cell.
   b. Another idea was to design a lighter car.
   c. A regular battery could push it faster and farther.

3. Which of the following should be the topic of your concept map?
   a. Electric Cars
   b. Early Electrics
   c. Modern Electrics

4. If you were to make a concept map for the section called "Some Progress," which of the following would be a supporting detail?
   a. Noel Perrin tried to drive cross-country in 1991.
   b. There is little chance that your next car will be an electric.
   c. Cars with gasoline engines also went fast.

5. If you made a concept map for the last section of the article, what would you list as the main idea?
   a. Road Tests
   b. Planning Ahead
   c. Electricity Pumps

Comprehension Check

Review the article if necessary. Then answer these questions:

1. Why do some people think the electric car is a good idea?
   a. because it is slower than a gas-driven car
   b. because it is cleaner than a gas-driven car
   c. because it is faster than a gas-driven car

2. When did the electric car and the steamer begin to be less popular than the gas-powered car?
   a. in 1912
   b. around 1900
   c. in the 1960s

3. What is the biggest problem that Noel Perrin faced on his trip in 1991?
   a. going up a steep hill
   b. recharging his car
   c. going on flat land

4. In 1992, how often did the truck pull into a charging station?
   a. about every 20 minutes
   b. about every 24 hours
   c. about every 60 miles

5. Why would nighttime be the best time to recharge electric cars?
   a. because there are more cars on the road during the night
   b. because electric companies have more than enough power at night
   c. because fuel pumps would create more pollution during the night

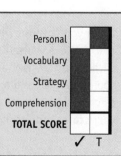

Check your answers with your teacher. Give yourself 1 point for each correct answer, and fill in your Strategy score here. Then turn to page 201 and transfer your score onto Graph 1.

Personal
Vocabulary
Strategy
Comprehension
TOTAL SCORE
✓ T

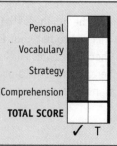

Check your answers with your teacher. Give yourself 1 point for each correct answer, and fill in your Comprehension score here. Then turn to page 201 and transfer your score onto Graph 1.

Personal
Vocabulary
Strategy
Comprehension
TOTAL SCORE
✓ T

Extending

Choose one or more of these activities:

RESEARCH AIR POLLUTION

Find out how air pollution might be affecting the weather. Use the resources on this page or ones you find yourself to answer some of these questions: What is the ozone layer? What is air pollution doing to it? How will this affect our weather? Share your findings with the class.

DESIGN AN AD

Design and create an ad for an electric car. You might draw a picture of a modern electric car. Or you might draw a picture showing the pollution caused by gasoline-powered cars. Be sure to include a clever slogan or caption for your ad.

CREATE A TIME LINE

Find out more about the history of electric cars. The resources listed on this page can help. If you'd like, list your findings on a time line.

Resources

Books

Coughlan, John. *Green Cars: Earth-Friendly Electric Vehicles.* Capstone Press, 1994.

Kahl, Jonathan D. W. *Hazy Skies: Weather and the Environment.* How's the Weather? Lerner Publications, 1997.

Miller, Christina G., and Louise A. Berry. *Air Alert: Rescuing the Earth's Atmosphere.* Atheneum, 1996.

Web Sites

http://www.care2.com/channels/ecoinfo/hybrid
This site contains a fact sheet describing hybrid cars and links to information about how hybrid cars benefit the environment and how they work.

http://www.ott.doe.gov/hev
This Web site contains up-to-date information on hybrid electric vehicles. It includes links to government, manufacturer, and technology sites.

apprehensively

awkwardly

calmly

carefully

loudly

proudly

shyly

swiftly

Listen to the Drumbeat

Building Background

In "Listen to the Drumbeat," Sara is given a chance to do something she's always wanted to do. What have you always dreamed of doing? Maybe you've dreamed of playing your favorite sport really well or performing on a stage. Maybe you've imagined yourself a famous person doing an important job. Think about what you have always wanted to do. Then write your feelings about it on the lines below.

_____

_____

_____

_____

_____

_____

_____

_____

CLIPBOARD

apprehensively
in a worried manner
(or way)

awkwardly

calmly

carefully

CLIPBOARD

loudly

proudly

shyly

swiftly

Vocabulary Builder

1. Each vocabulary word in the margin ends in the suffix -*ly*. A **suffix** is a word part that is added to the end of a word. Adding a suffix often changes the word's meaning and function. For example, adding the suffix -*ly* to the root word *sad* changes the adjective *sad* to an adverb meaning "in an unhappy manner, or way."

2. For each word on the clipboards, draw a line between the root word and the suffix. Then write what the word means with the suffix added. Use context clues from the story or a dictionary to help you figure out any unfamiliar words. The first one has been done for you.

3. Save your work. You will use it again in the Vocabulary Check.

Strategy Builder

Drawing Conclusions About Characters

- Every story is told from a particular point of view. The **point of view** reveals the thoughts and feelings of the **narrator**—the one who is telling the story. When the narrator is a character in the story, that story is told from a **first-person point of view**. A first-person narrator uses words such as *I, me, my,* and *mine* to tell the story.

- Sara is the first-person narrator in "Listen to the Drumbeat." She tells the story from her own point of view. That means that she can only tell what she is thinking and feeling. And she can only describe the events that she sees. She does not tell you everything about herself or the other characters, so you must draw your own conclusions about them.

- When you draw **conclusions** about a character, you make decisions about him or her. You can base your conclusions on clues from the story, such as what a particular character says or does. Or you can base your conclusions on what other characters say *to* or *about* that character.

Listen to the Drumbeat

by Nanette Larsen Dunford

As you read the first part of this story, see what conclusions you can draw about the characters. Use what they say and do to help you draw your conclusions.

"Race a dragon boat?" I said. "It's my dream! But . . ."

"But what, Sara? This is your chance!" exclaimed my cousin, Fa Ling. She waved her hand toward Hong Kong harbor. Many dragon boat racers were practicing for the famous Dragon Boat Festival to be held on the Fifth Day of the Fifth Moon.

"I don't even speak Chinese," I said.

"Just listen to the beat of the drum," Fa Ling said **calmly**.

I stood at the harbor's edge and watched the long, sleek dragon boats slice through the water. In each dragon boat stood a drummer. Forty boat-men paddled to the beat of his drum.

The beautiful boats with their painted dragon heads and red dragon tails didn't look at all like my canoe back home in America. I had always pretended my canoe was a dragon boat, and that I was a great dragon boat racer like my grandfather, Ng Yau.

The boats were coming closer now. The spray from hundreds of paddles looked as if dozens of dragons were spewing foam from their mouths and lashing the water with their tails.

"Soon we will see Grandfather's boat," said Fa Ling.

"Fa—Fa Ling," I stuttered. "I'm frightened to meet Grandfather."

"Frightened?" said Fa Ling. "You've always dreamed of meeting him."

"Maybe he will think I'm different," I said, worried. "He is Chinese. I am American."

"Sara!" scolded my cousin. "You will always be Chinese. Just because you were born in America. . . ."

"People here must think I'm odd. I look Chinese, yet I can hardly speak a word of the language."

"You're worrying over nothing," said Fa Ling.

⬣ **Stop here for the Strategy Break.**

Strategy Break

Use these questions to help you draw conclusions about Sara:

1. What two things does the story say that Sara has always dreamed of doing? _____

_____

_____

2. How does Sara feel about meeting her grandfather, and why? _____

_____

_____

3. What conclusions can you draw about Sara so far? _____

_____

_____

_____

4. How is Sara's personality different from Fa Ling's? _____

_____

_____

 Go on reading to see what happens.

Soon boatmen were clambering onto the docks. Suddenly, a small man was standing before me. He grinned widely.

"Grandfather, meet Sara," said Fa Ling.

Grandfather began shaking my hand vigorously.

"I am glad to meet you," I said slowly in Chinese.

"I am glad to meet you," he said slowly in English.

We both laughed and nodded our heads.

Grandfather motioned **proudly** to his dragon boat. He spoke to Fa Ling in Chinese. I was glad Fa Ling could speak both English and Chinese.

"Grandfather says he will be happy to take us in his dragon boat. He has heard you are a good canoeist," she translated.

I smiled **shyly**.

Walking toward his dragon boat, Grandfather spoke and Fa Ling translated his words. "Dragons have long been a symbol of China. The Dragon Boat Festival is in memory of a famous poet, Ch'u Yuan, who drowned in a river more than two thousand years ago. People rowed their dragon boats up and down the river trying to rescue him. But he was never found."

I stepped **carefully** into the dragon boat. It was narrow like a canoe. Yet my canoe back home didn't have green dragon scales painted on its body. The boatmen scrambled aboard. Grandfather sat next to me.

"Grandfather says to paddle to the rhythm of the drummer," said Fa Ling, smiling. "We're going to race that other dragon boat out to the buoy."

I clutched my paddle **apprehensively**. This was it. All my life, I had dreamed of racing a dragon boat with my grandfather. Now I was scared.

The drummer began to beat his drum **loudly**. The race was on. **Awkwardly**, I dipped my paddle. Our dragon boat swished through the water. But I didn't seem to be helping. My paddle was up when the other paddles were down. My paddle splashed the water as the other paddles rose.

Then I remembered: "Listen to the beat of the drum."

I concentrated hard on the drumbeat. Slowly, I began to feel the rhythm. Our dragon boat whisked more **swiftly** over Hong Kong harbor.

I looked at Grandfather sitting beside me. Our paddles were sliding into the water at the same instant. His dark eyes met mine. We smiled. There was no need to speak in Chinese or English. We were working together as one.

The feel of the wind and water on my face was exhilarating. Again and again, I thrust my paddle through the water to the beat of the drum. Faster and faster, our dragon boat skimmed over the harbor. I felt as if I were riding on the back of a fleet-footed dragon.

Suddenly the buoy loomed before us. We were in a dead heat with the other dragon boat. Our drummer pounded harder. We paddled faster. The ferocious-looking dragon head of our boat inched in front. We whizzed past the buoy. We had won! My teammates and I together let out a cheer.

Grandfather enthusiastically shook my hand. In slow English, he said, "Congratulations. You are a great dragon boat racer."

I beamed at him and replied in Chinese, "Thank you. You speak English very well."

His grin was the biggest yet. He turned to Fa Ling and spoke in Chinese.

"Grandfather says he's been practicing English words for weeks." Then Fa Ling winked. "He was afraid you might think he was odd if he didn't know even one English word."

I smiled and grabbed Grandfather's hand. No longer was I a Chinese from America and Grandfather a Chinese from Hong Kong. We were two dragon boat racers. Best of all, he was my grandfather and I was his grand-daughter. ●

Strategy Follow-up

Use these questions to help you draw conclusions about Sara:

1. How does Sara feel when she first gets into the dragon boat? _____

_____

_____

_____

_____

2. What happens when she concentrates on the drumbeat? _____

_____

_____

_____

_____

3. What conclusion can you draw about Sara's skill as a racer? _____

_____

_____

_____

_____

✓Personal Checklist

Read each question and put a check (✓) in the correct box.

1. How well do you understand why Sara is scared to take part in the dragon boat race?
   - ☐ 3 (extremely well)
   - ☐ 2 (fairly well)
   - ☐ 1 (not well)

2. How well do you understand why Sara and her grandfather are nervous about meeting each other?
   - ☐ 3 (extremely well)
   - ☐ 2 (fairly well)
   - ☐ 1 (not well)

3. How well did what you wrote in Building Background help you understand Sara's dream and her feelings about it?
   - ☐ 3 (extremely well)
   - ☐ 2 (fairly well)
   - ☐ 1 (not well)

4. In the Vocabulary Builder, how many words were you able to define correctly?
   - ☐ 3 (7–8 words)
   - ☐ 2 (4–6 words)
   - ☐ 1 (0–3 words)

5. In the Strategy Break and Follow-up, how well were you able to draw conclusions about Sara and Fa Ling?
   - ☐ 3 (extremely well)
   - ☐ 2 (fairly well)
   - ☐ 1 (not well)

Vocabulary Check

Look back at the work you did in the Vocabulary Builder. Then answer each question by circling the correct letter.

1. Which vocabulary word means "in a worried manner"?
   - a. awkwardly
   - b. apprehensively
   - c. carefully

2. Which word has the opposite meaning of *swiftly*?
   - a. slowly
   - b. quickly
   - c. immediately

3. Grandfather pointed proudly to his dragon boat. What does *proudly* mean?
   - a. in a very pleased manner
   - b in a very fast manner
   - c. in a very shy manner

4. Which vocabulary word means "in a quiet manner"?
   - a. swiftly
   - b. loudly
   - c. calmly

5. At the beginning of the race, Sara awkwardly dipped her paddle in the water. What does *awkwardly* mean?
   - a. in an excited manner
   - b. in a clumsy manner
   - c. in a careful manner

	Add the numbers that you just checked to get your Personal Checklist score. Fill in your score here. Then turn to page 201 and transfer your score onto Graph 1.		Personal		
			Vocabulary		
			Strategy		
			Comprehension		
			TOTAL SCORE		
				✓ T	

	Check your answers with your teacher. Give yourself 1 point for each correct answer, and fill in your Vocabulary score here. Then turn to page 201 and transfer your score onto Graph 1.		Personal		
			Vocabulary		
			Strategy		
			Comprehension		
			TOTAL SCORE		
				✓ T	

Strategy Check

Review what you wrote in the Strategy Break and Follow-up. Also review the rest of the story. Then answer these questions:

1. Which clue helped you conclude that Sara was frightened to meet her grandfather?

    a. "Race a dragon boat?" I said. "It's my dream."

    b. I had always pretended my canoe was a dragon boat.

    c. "Fa—Fa Ling," I stuttered.

2. What conclusion did you draw about Sara's skill as a racer?

    a. She must not like to race very much.

    b. She must not be a very good racer.

    c. She must be a very good racer.

3. Which clue helped you conclude that Fa Ling is different from Sara?

    a. She waved her hand toward Hong Kong harbor.

    b. "You're worrying over nothing," said Fa Ling.

    c. "Soon we will see Grandfather's boat," said Fa Ling.

4. Which clue helped you conclude that Grandfather was nervous about meeting Sara?

    a. Grandfather enthusiastically shook my hand.

    b. His grin was the biggest yet.

    c. "Grandfather says he's been practicing English words for weeks."

5. Based on the last paragraph of the story, what can you conclude about Sara?

    a. She doesn't feel nervous anymore about meeting her grandfather.

    b. She still feels nervous about meeting her grandfather.

    c. She will always feel nervous when she's around her grandfather.

Comprehension Check

Review the story if necessary. Then answer these questions:

1. What has Sara always dreamed of doing?

    a. riding in a canoe

    b. racing a dragon boat

    c. going to China

2. Sara says that people in China must think she is odd. Why does she say that?

    a. because she has never raced in a Chinese dragon boat

    b. because she speaks Chinese but doesn't look Chinese

    c. because she looks Chinese but doesn't speak Chinese

3. At the beginning of the race, where is Sara's paddle when the other paddles are down?

    a. in the dragon boat

    b. down in the water

    c. up in the air

4. What helps Sara paddle in time with everyone else?

    a. her grandfather's smile

    b. the beat of the drum

    c. the feel of the wind and water on her face

5. At the end of the race, why does Sara grab her grandfather's hand?

    a. because she's happy to be his granddaughter

    b. because they lost the race and she's afraid

    c. because his English is better than she thought

Check your answers with your teacher. Give yourself 1 point for each correct answer, and fill in your Strategy score here. Then turn to page 201 and transfer your score onto Graph 1.

Personal
Vocabulary
Strategy
Comprehension
TOTAL SCORE
✓ T

Check your answers with your teacher. Give yourself 1 point for each correct answer, and fill in your Comprehension score here. Then turn to page 201 and transfer your score onto Graph 1.

Personal
Vocabulary
Strategy
Comprehension
TOTAL SCORE
✓ T

Extending

Choose one or both of these activities:

DRAW A DRAGON BOAT

Draw or paint a picture of Grandfather's dragon boat. Use descriptions of the boat in the story to help you. You might draw the boat by itself. Or you might draw a picture of the boat in the middle of a race. If you'd like, draw Sara, Fa Ling, Grandfather, the boatmen, and the drummer in the boat.

FIND OUT ABOUT DRAGONS AND CHINA

Research to find out more about dragons and China. Use the books listed on this page if you'd like. Try to answer the following questions. Then share your findings with your class.

- What does the dragon represent in China?

- What are some traditional Chinese beliefs about dragons?

- What powers are dragons believed to have?

- What role does the dragon play in the Chinese New Year?

Resources

Books

Austin, Judith M. *The Chinese New Year Dragon.* Globalfriends Adventure Series. Globalfriends Collection, 1997.

Cohen, Shari. *Draw Fantasy: Dragons, Centaurs, and Other Mythological Characters.* Lowell House, 1997.

Learning New Words

VOCABULARY

From Lesson 11
• snugly

From Lesson 13
• gleefully

From Lesson 15
• apprehensively
• awkwardly
• calmly
• carefully
• loudly
• proudly
• shyly
• swiftly

From Lesson 13
• championship

Suffixes

A suffix is a word part that is added to the end of a root word. When you add a suffix, you often change the root word's meaning and function. For example, the suffix *-less* means "without," so the root word *fear* changes from a noun to an adjective meaning "without fear."

-ly

The suffix *-ly* means "in a _____ way, or manner." All of the vocabulary words in "Listen to the Drumbeat" end in *-ly.* They are adverbs that describe the ways in which the characters felt, spoke, or acted.

Write the definition of each word.

1. cheerfully _____

2. sadly _____

3. excitedly _____

4. slowly _____

5. smoothly _____

-ship

The suffix *-ship* can have different meanings. It can mean "quality or condition of being _____." Or it can mean "position, title, or job of _____."

In the story "Derby," Quincy wins the championship with his Thumbtack Special. In this case, *championship* means "position or title of champion."

Write the word that each definition describes.

1. position or title of member _____

2. quality of being sportsmanlike _____

3. condition of being related _____

4. condition of being a partner _____

5. position or title of governor _____

Prefixes

A prefix is a word part that is added to the beginning of a root word. (*Pre-* means "before.") When you add a prefix, you often change the root word's meaning and function. For example, the prefix *un-* means "not," so adding *un-* to the root word *believable* changes it to its antonym, *unbelievable.*

dis-

The prefix *dis-* can mean "opposite of," "lack of," or "not." In "Derby," Quincy's dad's car is disqualified from the race. *Disqualified* means "not qualified" to compete in the race.

Write the word that describes each definition below.

1. not honest _____

2. opposite of being engaged _____

3. opposite of being connected _____

4. not approved (of) _____

5. lack of comfort _____

6. lack of ability _____

re-

The prefix *re-* means "again." In Lesson 14 you learned that one of the drawbacks of electric cars is that their batteries must be recharged too often. *Recharged* means "charged again." Researchers are working on ways to make electric cars better. Can you figure out what the word *research* means?

Write the definition of each word.

1. research _____

2. rethink _____

3. reheat _____

4. repaint _____

5. rewind _____

6. rewrite _____

VOCABULARY

From Lesson 13
• disqualified

From Lesson 14
• recharged

LESSON **16** Colorblind

Building Background

You've probably heard of colorblindness, but do you know what it is? Does being colorblind mean that you can't see any colors at all? Do you know what causes colorblindness? Get together with a partner. Talk about these questions and others that you might have about colorblindness. Then write down at least three of your questions on the lines below. After you finish reading "Colorblind," get back together with your partner and reread your questions. Use what you learned in the article to answer them.

_____

_____

_____

_____

_____

_____

_____

cones

optic nerve

pupil

retina

rods

visual cortex

Vocabulary Builder

1. "Colorblind" uses several specialized vocabulary words. As you know, **specialized vocabulary** words are all related to a particular topic. For example, the specialized vocabulary words in the margin are all related to the human eye.

2. It can be hard to understand specialized vocabulary words when you read about them. Sometimes looking at a diagram helps. The **diagram** on page 157 is a drawing of an eye. As you read the article, label the parts of the eye and complete the sentences with specialized vocabulary words. Use descriptions and the context clues in the article to help you figure out where the words belong.

3. Save your work. You will use it again in the Vocabulary Check.

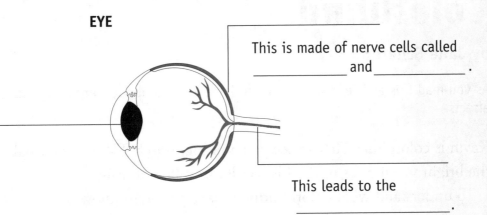

EYE

This is made of nerve cells called
_____ and_____ .

This leads to the
_____ .

Strategy Builder

Identifying Causes and Effects

- "Colorblind" tells about some of the causes and effects of color-blindness. **Cause-and-effect** writing is used to explain how one event causes another event. For example, deep puddles are a result of a heavy rainfall. In this case, the heavy rainfall is the cause. The deep puddles are the effect, or result, of the rainfall.

- When you look for causes and effects, you need to be careful. An event may follow another event but may not be the result of that event. Use the "because" test to help you figure out if one event is the result of another. For instance, imagine that you went out to play after you ate lunch. You didn't go out to play *because* you ate lunch. That event just happened *after* you ate lunch.

- You can list causes and effects on **cause-and-effect links**. The cause-and-effect links below show what happens when you don't brush your teeth.

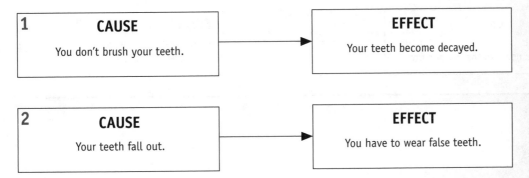

1 **CAUSE**	**EFFECT**
You don't brush your teeth.	Your teeth become decayed.

2 **CAUSE**	**EFFECT**
Your teeth fall out.	You have to wear false teeth.

- As you read this article, you will use cause-and-effect links to list some of the causes and effects of colorblindness.

Colorblind

by Jane Scherer

As you read this article, apply what you have learned about identifying causes and effects.

Kevin is colorblind. He can see you and me, watch TV, and play ball, but the bright green grass under his feet looks yellow to him.

To understand what colorblindness is, you have to know how the human eye works. Light comes into the eye through the **pupil**—the small, dark hole in the center. The light passes through a lens that focuses it and sends it into the back of the eyeball. This part of the eye is called the **retina**. It contains special cells that are light-sensitive.

When you look at something, the cells in your retina send chemical signals to your brain. Those signals travel along the **optic nerve** to the **visual cortex**, the part of your brain that is in charge of seeing. There, the nerve signals are translated into the image of a house, a car, or your sister.

⬣ **Stop here for the Strategy Break.**

Strategy Break

If you were to use cause-and-effect links to show what happens when you look at something, your links might look like this:

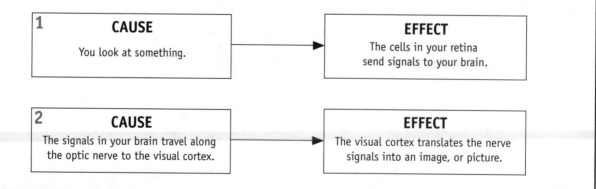

➡ Go on reading.

The retina has millions of nerve cells. Some are called **rods**. Others are called **cones**. Go into a darkish room and look around. The 100 million rods in each eye are sensitive in dim light, and make adjustments so that you can see even if there isn't too much light.

When there's not much light, however, everything looks gray. This is because the seven million cone cells in each eye—which are sensitive to different colors—can see color only in bright light. That's why shocking pink, orange, and other bright colors look gray in dim light.

There are three different types of cone cells. Each is "in charge" of a different color: red, green, or blue. Your brain combines these three basic colors into the rainbow of shades that make up our world. When you look at a STOP sign, your red cones react. You know the sign is red. Joey is colorblind to red because he is missing certain cone cells. He can see blue and green fine, but not red.

When all three types of cone cells are missing, the person sees only black, white, and shades of gray. However, not too many people are totally colorblind. Not being able to tell red from green is much more common.

Babies are born naturally colorblind. Their cone cells haven't developed yet. It takes six to eight months before a baby will be attracted to colorful toys and pictures.

More men than women tend to be colorblind. In the United States, about eight out of every one hundred men are colorblind. One in every two hundred women is, too. It's something you inherit from your parents—like the color of your hair or eyes. If both of them have trouble with a certain color, you are more likely to have trouble, too.

Kids like Kevin and Joey may not even know they are blind to certain colors. This can cause problems when it comes to picking out clothes. Kevin might think a green shirt is gray. Joey might insist HIS red shirt is green. Otherwise, colorblindness isn't too hard to live with.

Eye doctors have special vision tests to find out if someone is colorblind. They are flash cards that show letters, numbers, or images made up of dots. The dots on one card might be green surrounded by red. A person blind to green won't be able to read the figures in the test. All that he or she will see are a bunch of red dots.

There's nothing that can be done to "fix" colorblindness. It doesn't cause any pain, and it isn't dangerous. Kevin and Joey will just have to learn other ways to recognize such things as traffic lights and color-coded signals, and that isn't really hard to do. ●

Strategy Follow-up

First go back and answer the questions that you and your partner wrote in Building Background. Then fill in the missing cause-and-effect links below. Review the article if necessary.

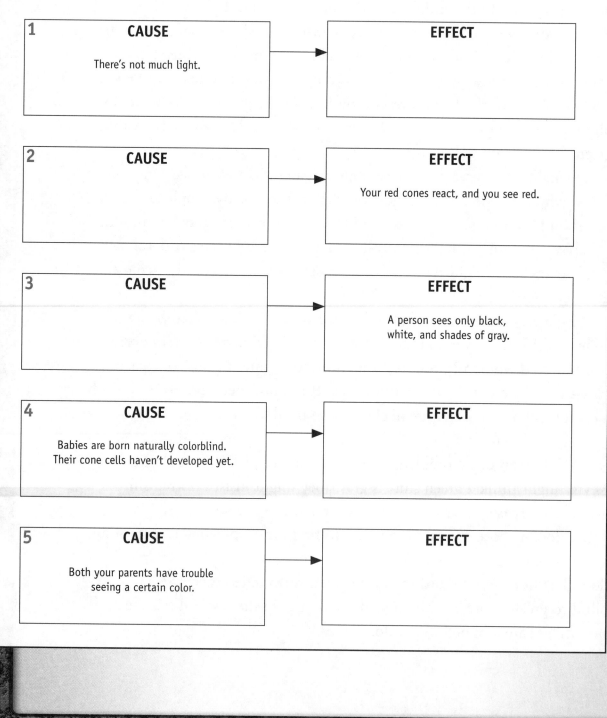

1   **CAUSE**

There's not much light.

EFFECT

2   **CAUSE**

EFFECT

Your red cones react, and you see red.

3   **CAUSE**

EFFECT

A person sees only black, white, and shades of gray.

4   **CAUSE**

Babies are born naturally colorblind. Their cone cells haven't developed yet.

EFFECT

5   **CAUSE**

Both your parents have trouble seeing a certain color.

EFFECT

✓Personal Checklist

Read each question and put a check (✓) in the correct box.

1. How well do you understand the information in "Colorblind"?

   ☐ 3 (extremely well)

   ☐ 2 (fairly well)

   ☐ 1 (not well)

2. How well do you understand the connection between cone cells and seeing colors?

   ☐ 3 (extremely well)

   ☐ 2 (fairly well)

   ☐ 1 (not well)

3. When you finished this article, how well were you able to answer the questions that you listed in Building Background?

   ☐ 3 (extremely well)

   ☐ 2 (fairly well)

   ☐ 1 (not well)

4. In the Vocabulary Builder, how many specialized vocabulary words were you able to use correctly on the diagram?

   ☐ 3 (5–6 words)

   ☐ 2 (3–4 words)

   ☐ 1 (0–2 words)

5. In the Strategy Follow-up, how well were you able to identify the missing causes and effects?

   ☐ 3 (extremely well)

   ☐ 2 (fairly well)

   ☐ 1 (not well)

Vocabulary Check

Look back at the work you did in the Vocabulary Builder. Then answer each question by circling the correct letter.

1. What is the back of the eyeball called?

   a. visual cortex

   b. pupil

   c. retina

2. Which of the following is located in the brain?

   a. visual cortex

   b. cones

   c. rods

3. Light comes in through the small, dark hole in the center of the eye. What is that part of the eye called?

   a. rod

   b. pupil

   c. optic nerve

4. The retina is made of two kinds of nerve cells. What are they called?

   a. rods and pupil

   b. optic nerve and cones

   c. rods and cones

5. When you look at something, cells in your retina send chemical signals to your brain. Along what do those signals travel?

   a. optic nerve

   b. visual cortex

   c. rods

Add the numbers that you just checked to get your Personal Checklist score. Fill in your score here. Then turn to page 201 and transfer your score onto Graph 1.

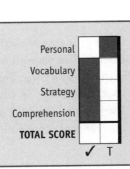

Check your answers with your teacher. Give yourself 1 point for each correct answer, and fill in your Vocabulary score here. Then turn to page 201 and transfer your score onto Graph 1.

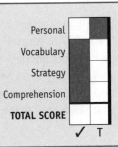

Strategy Check

Review the cause-and-effect links that you completed in the Strategy Follow-up. Then answer these questions:

1. What causes babies to take six to eight months before they are attracted to colorful toys and pictures?

    a. The babies' parents are colorblind too.

    b. Babies can only see black, white, and gray.

    c. Their cone cells aren't developed when they're born.

2. If you are not colorblind, what happens when you look at a STOP sign?

    a. Your red cones react, and you see the color red.

    b. Your red cones react, and you see the color green.

    c. Your red cones react, and you see the color blue.

3. What is the most likely effect if both your parents have trouble seeing a certain color?

    a. You'll have trouble seeing it, too.

    b. You will be totally colorblind.

    c. You won't have any colorblindness.

4. What causes a person to see only black, white, and shades of gray?

    a. The red cones are missing.

    b. The red and green cones are missing.

    c. All three types of cones are missing.

5. What happens when you look around a room that doesn't have very much light?

    a. You can see colors very well.

    b. Everything looks gray.

    c. Everything looks red.

Comprehension Check

Review the article if necessary. Then answer these questions:

1. What happens when nerve signals from the eye are translated in the brain?

    a. You see an image of what you're looking at.

    b. You can't see any colors.

    c. You see only red and green.

2. How old are babies when they start to see colors?

    a. six to eight weeks old

    b. six to eight months old

    c. about a year old

3. Who is more likely to be colorblind, your father or your mother?

    a. Your father is more likely.

    b. Your mother is more likely.

    c. The chance is the same for both.

4. If you were blind to green, what colors would you see when you looked at a traffic light?

    a. green and red

    b. red and yellow

    c. green and yellow

5. How do people who are colorblind deal with their condition?

    a. They always cross the street with someone else.

    b. They have doctors cure their colorblindness.

    c. They learn ways to recognize the colors they can't see.

Check your answers with your teacher. Give yourself 1 point for each correct answer, and fill in your Strategy score here. Then turn to page 201 and transfer your score onto Graph 1.

Personal	
Vocabulary	
Strategy	
Comprehension	
TOTAL SCORE	✓ T

Check your answers with your teacher. Give yourself 1 point for each correct answer, and fill in your Comprehension score here. Then turn to page 201 and transfer your score onto Graph 1.

Personal	
Vocabulary	
Strategy	
Comprehension	
TOTAL SCORE	✓ T

Extending

Choose one or more of these activities:

DRAW A MODEL OF A HUMAN EYE

Use the diagram in the Vocabulary Builder and the resources on this page to help you make your own drawing of an eye. Label the parts of the eye that you already know. Then research to find out the names of other parts, and label those on your drawing. Display your drawing in your classroom. Then tell a fact about each part of the eye that you have labeled.

LIST WAYS TO DEAL WITH COLORBLINDNESS

The author of this article says that people who are colorblind have to learn other ways to recognize some colors. Make a list of ways that people can recognize the colors in things such as traffic lights and train crossings. Compare your list with a partner's.

RESEARCH HOW ANIMALS SEE

Find out how and what animals see. Can some animals see better than humans? Are there any animals that are naturally colorblind? How are an animal's eyes different from a person's? Uncover some fun facts and share them with your class. Use the resources on this page if you need help in getting started.

Resources

Books

Doherty, Paul, Don Rathjen, and the Exploratorium Teacher Institute. *The Cheshire Cat and Other Eye-Popping Experiments on How We See the World.* Exploratorium Science Snackbook Series. John Wiley & Sons, 1995.

Dossenbach, Monika, and Hans D. Dossenbach. *Eyeopeners! All About Animal Vision.* Blackbirch Marketing, 1998.

Llamas, Andreu. *Sight.* The Five Senses of the Animal World. Chelsea House Publishers, 1996.

Web Sites

http://cvs.anu.edu.au/andy/beye/beyehome.html
This site lets you see the world through a bee's eyes.

http://www.kidshealth.org/kid/talk/qa/color_blind.html
This site answers questions about what color blindness is, who is more likely to be color blind, and why.

http://www.yorku.ca/eye/eye1.htm
This Web site explains all the parts of the eye. It includes a clearly labeled diagram of the eye.

LESSON 17 Picturing the World: The Adventures of a Professional Photographer

Building Background

In "Picturing the World," Jodi Cobb answers an interviewer's questions about her experiences as a photographer. If you could interview anyone who has ever lived, who would it be, and why? Pick someone you'd like to interview, and then think about the questions that you would ask him or her. Write at least four of those questions on the lines below.

Q: _____

_____

Q: _____

_____

Q: _____

_____

Q: _____

_____

Q: _____

_____

Vocabulary Builder

1. Each boldfaced vocabulary word below is followed by three other words. Two of the three words are synonyms of the boldfaced word. One word is an antonym. (Reminder: **Synonyms** are words with the same meaning. **Antonyms** have opposite meanings.)

2. For any boldfaced word that you already know, circle the antonym that does not belong. Then, as you read the interview, use context to help you figure out the other boldfaced words. Return to this exercise and circle the rest of the antonyms.

avoid	meet	dodge	escape
flashy	showy	dull	bright
forbidden	banned	approved	disallowed
genuine	fake	real	true
immediate	instant	delayed	now
invisible	unobserved	unseen	noticed
offensive	nasty	insulting	pleasing
respectful	impolite	courteous	well-behaved
submissive	obedient	agreeable	proud
threat	danger	safety	risk

avoid

flashy

forbidden

genuine

immediate

invisible

offensive

respectful

submissive

threat

Strategy Builder

How to Read an Interview

- An **interview** is like a conversation. One person asks **questions**, and the other person gives **answers**. The person who asks the questions is called the **interviewer**.

- The purpose of an interview is to **inform** the reader. The interviewer in "Picturing the World" wants to inform readers about Jodi and her adventures in other countries. To get the most out of an interview, an interviewer asks questions that will provide information—not just "yes" or "no" answers. To get the most interesting information, interviewers often ask questions that begin with *Who, What, Where, When, Why,* and *How.*

- As you read the interview, you also will answer *Who, What, Where, When, Why,* and *How* questions about what you have learned.

Picturing the World: The Adventures of a Professional Photographer

by Allison Lassieur

Grunting camels, strange foods, exotic countries, and extraordinary people—Jodi Cobb has seen them all and more as a photographer with *National Geographic* magazine. Since 1978 Jodi has worked in more than twenty-five countries, written many books, and taken thousands of pictures. In this interview, she tells about her experiences.

Q: You lived overseas as a child. How did that influence your decision to become a photographer?

Jodi: I'd been around the world twice by the time I was twelve, and I had a sense of the amazing variety of cultures and people. As an adult, I just had to get back out there and explore.

What inspired you to become a photographer?

In my senior year of college I took a photo class. I discovered that photography is **immediate**—I could see the reaction when people looked at a photograph. Photography goes right to the mind and heart.

⬡ **Stop here for the Strategy Break.**

Strategy Break

Use what you've learned so far to answer these questions:

Q: Who is being interviewed? _____

Q: What does she do? _____
_____

Q: Why does she do this job? _____
_____
_____

Go on reading.

What was your most interesting story?

The most interesting story I did for the *Geographic* was "The Women of Saudi Arabia." These women are **invisible** to the outside world because photography of them is **forbidden** in their culture. I did the story on them and their lives behind the veil.

As an American, how are you treated by people in other cultures?

It varies. In cultures where women have a **submissive** role I'm not taken seriously at all, which can be good in getting me into situations. Because I'm not a **threat**, I get invited into people's homes and into their lives.

What do you do to prepare for an assignment?

I read as much as I can on a place and learn about local customs. For example, it's an insult to show the soles of your feet in the Arab world. So, to sit with your legs crossed is just horrible. To pat Thai children on the head is an insult. It's a spiritual thing about the head being sacred.

What strange foods have you eaten?

My most unusual meal was in a remote Chinese village where they brought me fried bumblebees.

How was it?

I cried. I had been waiting in this little village for three days because it was raining and the planes wouldn't fly. At the end of the third day I came back to the hotel, and that's what they served me. I started to cry, and my guide told them, "She is overwhelmed by your generosity." After that she told me that every food they served me was chicken.

Did you eat it after that?

Yes. I've learned to chew without tasting.

What about unusual transportation?

Let's see, I've gone by camel in Jordan, by elephant in Thailand, by ice-breaker across the Baltic Sea in Russia, by gondola in Venice, by helicopter, and by horseback.

Which did you like best?

Oh, I liked the camels. It's a very rocking motion, and their faces are just wonderful. They're so arrogant. They make the most amazing noises when they walk. They just groan, grunt, and moan every step of the way, like they're complaining the whole time. It was fun.

Is there one object that you find useful wherever you go?

A Swiss Army knife. I had my own chopsticks in China. Most diseases in China are transmitted through chopsticks. A way to **avoid** illnesses is to carry your own plastic ones with you.

Do you dress in the clothing of the culture you're visiting?
Wherever I am, I try to dress as much like the people I'm photographing as possible. I don't want a wall between me and the people. So if people find blue jeans **offensive** I don't wear blue jeans. When I'm working in very poor countries I don't wear **flashy** clothes.

Do you have any tricks that you use to help people accept you and your work?
A smile! A smile and a **respectful** attitude go a long way. It's amazing. If you come barging in, elbows flying, you're going to get that in return. If you come in respectful of their culture with a **genuine** curiosity about their lives, people know that. ●

Strategy Follow-up

Review the interview if necessary. Then answer these questions:

Q: Where has Jodi Cobb traveled as a photographer? _____
_____
_____

Q: What does Jodi do before she visits a foreign country?_____
_____
_____

Q: Why does being a woman sometimes help Jodi in her work?_____
_____
_____

Q: Who doesn't take her seriously?_____
_____
_____

Q: When did she get so upset that she cried?_____
_____
_____

Q: How does Jodi get people to accept and talk to her? _____
_____
_____

✓Personal Checklist

Read each question and put a check (✓) in the correct box.

1. How well do you understand why Jodi Cobb became a photographer?
   - ☐ 3 (extremely well)
   - ☐ 2 (fairly well)
   - ☐ 1 (not well)

2. How well do you understand why she loves her job?
   - ☐ 3 (extremely well)
   - ☐ 2 (fairly well)
   - ☐ 1 (not well)

3. How well did the questions that you wrote in Building Background help prepare you for reading and understanding this interview?
   - ☐ 3 (extremely well)
   - ☐ 2 (fairly well)
   - ☐ 1 (not well)

4. In the Vocabulary Builder, how well were you able to identify the antonyms that did not belong?
   - ☐ 3 (extremely well)
   - ☐ 2 (fairly well)
   - ☐ 1 (not well)

5. How well were you able to answer the questions in the Strategy Break and Follow-up?
   - ☐ 3 (extremely well)
   - ☐ 2 (fairly well)
   - ☐ 1 (not well)

Vocabulary Check

Look back at the work you did in the Vocabulary Builder. Then answer each question by circling the correct letter.

1. Which word does not have the same meaning as *avoid*?
   a. meet
   b. dodge
   c. escape

2. Which word does not have the same meaning as *immediate*?
   a. instant
   b. delayed
   c. now

3. Which vocabulary word means "not allowed"?
   a. forbidden
   b. invisible
   c. submissive

4. Which word does not have the same meaning as *threat*?
   a. danger
   b. safety
   c. risk

5. Which vocabulary word means the opposite of *respectful*?
   a. genuine
   b. flashy
   c. offensive

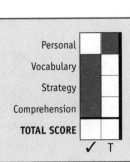

Add the numbers that you just checked to get your Personal Checklist score. Fill in your score here. Then turn to page 201 and transfer your score onto Graph 1.

Check your answers with your teacher. Give yourself 1 point for each correct answer, and fill in your Vocabulary score here. Then turn to page 201 and transfer your score onto Graph 1.

Strategy Check

Review the answers that you wrote in the Strategy Break and Follow-up. Then answer these questions:

1. What does Jodi Cobb do before she visits a foreign country?

   a. She dresses in flashy clothes.

   b. She packs a pair of plastic chopsticks.

   c. She reads about the place and its customs.

2. Which word would you use to begin a question about the places that Jodi has visited?

   a. How

   b. Where

   c. When

3. Which word would you use to begin a question about the reason Jodi became a photographer?

   a. Who

   b. When

   c. Why

4. Which word would you use to begin a question about the ways Jodi gets people to talk to her?

   a. How

   b. When

   c. Where

5. Who doesn't take Jodi seriously?

   a. the people in Thailand

   b. the people in China

   c. the people in cultures where women have a submissive role

Comprehension Check

Review the interview if necessary. Then answer these questions:

1. Which story does Jodi Cobb believe is her most interesting one?

   a. her story about food in China

   b. her story about the women of Saudi Arabia

   c. her story about camels in Jordan

2. Which of the following is considered insulting behavior in Thailand?

   a. patting a child on the head

   b. showing the soles of your feet

   c. wearing blue jeans

3. Why do you think Jodi's guide told the hotel people in China that Jodi was overwhelmed by their generosity?

   a. The guide didn't understand English very well.

   b. The guide thought that Jodi loved fried bumblebees.

   c. The guide didn't want to hurt their feelings.

4. Why doesn't Jodi wear flashy clothes when she works in poor countries?

   a. She doesn't want to stand out or offend anyone.

   b. She feels more comfortable in blue jeans anyway.

   c. Flashy clothes are very difficult for her to work in.

5. What does Jodi do to gain people's trust?

   a. She brings her own chopsticks.

   b. She smiles and respects the people she meets.

   c. She chews without tasting her food.

Check your answers with your teacher. Give yourself 1 point for each correct answer, and fill in your Strategy score here. Then turn to page 201 and transfer your score onto Graph 1.

Personal		
Vocabulary		
Strategy		
Comprehension		
TOTAL SCORE	✓	T

Check your answers with your teacher. Give yourself 1 point for each correct answer, and fill in your Comprehension score here. Then turn to page 201 and transfer your score onto Graph 1.

Personal		
Vocabulary		
Strategy		
Comprehension		
TOTAL SCORE	✓	T

Extending

Choose one or more of these activities:

INTERVIEW A FAMILY MEMBER

Interview an older family member. You could ask him or her about your own childhood. Some of your questions might include the following: Whom do I most look like in the family? What is your first memory of me? Or you might ask about your family's past. Some questions might include the following: Where were my grandparents born? How were holidays and special occasions celebrated before I was born? Prepare your list of questions before the interview. Be sure to use *Who, What, Where, When, Why,* and *How* questions.

RESEARCH CUSTOMS IN OTHER CULTURES

Using the resources on this page or ones you find yourself, learn more about the customs of Saudi Arabia, Thailand, or China. For example, you might find out about the traditional celebrations in one of these countries. Or you might learn about a country's traditional foods. Share your findings with your class. If possible, bring in pictures that illustrate the information you find.

DRAW PICTURES OF CAMELS

Draw two pictures of camels. Draw one picture of a camel with one hump. Then draw another picture of a camel with two humps. Find out what each kind of camel is called, and label your pictures. Use the resources on this page if you need help.

Resources

Books

Chiarelli, Brunetto, Anna Lisa Bebi, and A. B. Chiarelli. *The Atlas of World Cultures.* Peter Bedrick Books, 2001.

Garcia, Eulalia. *Camels: Ships of the Desert.* Secrets of the Animal World. Gareth Stevens, 1996.

Web Sites

http://www.arab.net/camels/welcome.html
This Web site contains interesting facts about camels.

http://www.camels-camels.com
This site contains information on camels as well as pictures of the two kinds of camels.

LESSON 18 Bugs for Dinner

Building Background

The selection you are about to read tells about the Pilgrims' voyage to America. The Pilgrims were the first British settlers of New England. They left their homes in Great Britain to find religious freedom in America. The ship that brought the Pilgrims to America was called the *Mayflower*. The *Mayflower* left Great Britain in August 1620 and arrived in what is now Plymouth, Massachusetts, in December. As you will discover when you read "Bugs for Dinner," life aboard the *Mayflower* was full of challenges.

Life was also very hard for the Pilgrims once they reached America. During their first winter, more than half of the Pilgrims died from the terrible cold. However, the future looked brighter in the summer of 1621. Looking forward to a good corn harvest, the Pilgrims planned a harvest festival in the fall. They celebrated the festival for three days and ate ducks, geese, and turkeys. About 90 Native Americans also went to the festival and brought along five deer. That festival became known as Thanksgiving Day. It soon spread to other New England colonies.

delicious

moldy

nibbled

preserved

spoiled

stale

Vocabulary Builder

1. All of the words in the margin have something to do with food. Complete each sentence below with one of the words. Use the context clues in the sentences to help you.

   a. Tiny bits of the muffin are gone because a mouse _____ on it.

   b. When food is _____, it tastes really good.

   c. Green growth on a piece of cheese means that it is _____.

   d. That loaf of bread is old, hard, and _____.

e. Food lasts a lot longer when it is _____.

f. We have to throw these vegetables away because they have

_____.

2. Save your work. You will use it again in the Vocabulary Check.

Strategy Builder

How to Read a Description

- When writing a **description**, an author uses **details** to create word pictures. These word pictures help readers "see" and understand things more clearly by appealing to the five senses. For example, in the selection you are about to read, the author uses many details to describe the Pilgrims' voyage on the *Mayflower.* She describes how things looked, sounded, felt, smelled, and tasted.

- Authors don't always have the same **purpose** when they write descriptions. For example, suppose an author described a new puppy's funny behavior. That author's purpose would probably be to **entertain** readers. In "Bugs for Dinner," however, the author's main purpose is to **inform**. She wants to let readers know what life was like on the *Mayflower.*

- When you read a description, you can use a **concept map** to keep track of the descriptive details. The following concept map contains the details that one author used to describe a scene at the beach. Notice that each detail appeals to a different sense.

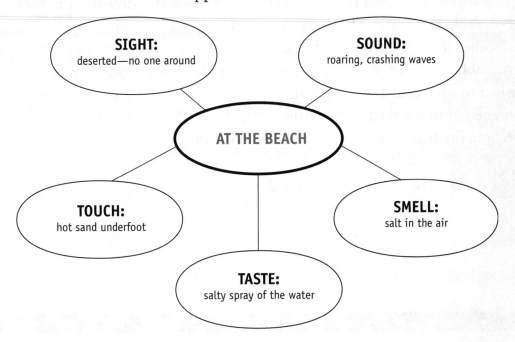

Bugs for Dinner

by Lucille Recht Penner

As you read the beginning of this selection, apply what you learned about reading a description. Pay special attention to the details that the author uses to describe the main cabin. Think about which senses they appeal to.

For sixty-six days the Pilgrims sailed across the Atlantic Ocean. The wind howled. The waves crashed against the sides of the little, crowded wooden boat. It was always noisy.

Inside the boat, people moaned, coughed, and shouted to make themselves heard against the roar of the wind and the creaking of sails. They were always cold and wet. Spray from the big ocean waves soaked everything on deck. Soon their clothes became stiff with salt left by the seawater.

There were a hundred and two passengers. Most of them slept crowded together in the main cabin. The ceiling was low. Anyone over five feet tall had to walk bent over. Each person had only a tiny space in which to sleep, prepare food, eat, wash, and pile all his or her belongings.

And everyone had tried to bring enough things to last a lifetime! Blankets, rugs, pillows, quilts, sheets, furniture, boxes of clothes and linens, dishes, tools, guns, armor, cradles, pots, pans, and special keepsakes were piled up to the ceiling. The cabin was jammed! It was hard for anyone even to move in there. And it smelled terrible.

Hardly anybody washed—there wasn't enough fresh water. And even people who washed their hands and faces didn't wash their clothes. Most people never changed at all. They wore the same clothes for the whole trip. The Pilgrims scratched and scratched, because lice and fleas lived in everyone's clothes and hair. There was no way to get rid of them.

Besides human beings and bugs, the *Mayflower* carried other passengers. Live rabbits, chickens, geese, and ducks were kept in a rowboat that was lashed to the deck. There were also pigs, goats, and sheep on board. But no one got to eat them. The settlers hoped that these few animals would become the parents of large flocks and herds in America.

⬣ **Stop here for the Strategy Break.**

Strategy Break

If you were to make a concept map of details that describe the main cabin, your map might look like this:

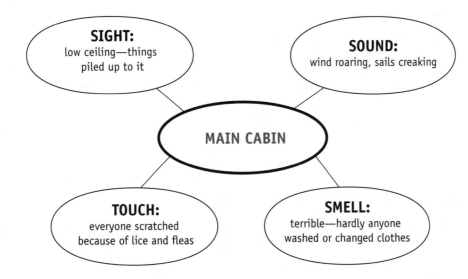

SIGHT:
low ceiling—things piled up to it

SOUND:
wind roaring, sails creaking

MAIN CABIN

TOUCH:
everyone scratched because of lice and fleas

SMELL:
terrible—hardly anyone washed or changed clothes

As you continue reading, notice the details that the author uses to describe the food that the Pilgrims ate on the *Mayflower*. You will use some of those details to create a concept map of your own.

➡ **Go on reading.**

What *did* the Pilgrims eat during their long voyage? Most of the food on the *Mayflower* was cold and dry. There were **moldy** cheese and dried peas. Salty beef and dried fish.

And there were ship's biscuits—as hard as rocks. Hundreds of these biscuits had been carried onto the boat before it sailed. They were stacked in huge piles. Ship's biscuits were made of wheat flour, pea flour, and water. They were flat and round, the size of dinner plates. The **stale** biscuits were almost impossible to chew. But somehow people sucked and **nibbled** them down.

Cheese was different. It didn't get as hard as the biscuits. Instead, the cheese quickly turned green and moldy.

Dried peas were stored in sacks so the mice and rats that dashed all over the ship wouldn't eat them. The settlers ate some of the peas on board, saving the rest to eat when they got to America.

There were also sacks of turnips, parsnips, onions, and cabbages. Vegetables kept pretty well. They just got a little hard on the outside and a little soft on the inside.

Some days the Pilgrims ate smoked herring or dried, salted codfish. Other days they had pork or beef. Because fresh meat would have **spoiled** quickly, the Pilgrims' meat was **preserved** in salt and packed in barrels. One of their favorite meats was neat's tongue—the tongue of an ox. They brought big boxes of dried ox tongues to eat on the trip.

Other boxes held spices—ginger, cinnamon, mace, cloves, nutmeg, and green ginger. These were very expensive, but the Pilgrims loved spicy food. And spices could cover up the bad taste of food that had begun to rot.

To wash down their salty, spicy meals, the Pilgrims drank beer, ale, wine, and even gin and brandy. They hated water. Even children drank beer.

Everyone on the *Mayflower* needed to drink often. When a family crouched around its mattress at mealtime, it was usually looking at cold, dry, salty food. But sometimes it was better not to look. Rats and cockroaches were all over. Little insects—weevils, maggots, and grubs—chewed tunnels into the ship's biscuits. Some of the Pilgrims preferred to eat at night. In the dark, they couldn't see the bugs crawling on their food.

Once in a while, each family got a treat: the chance to cook a hot dinner. Cooking usually wasn't allowed on the *Mayflower*. A stray spark could start a fire that might burn up the whole ship. But there were three small, iron boxes filled with sand for people to cook in. These were called fireboxes. The settlers took turns using them.

Sometimes they made labscouse—a thick soup of dried peas mixed with water and chunks of salty beef. The hot soup tasted **delicious**. And you could dip your hard biscuit into the soup to soften it. Little fat dumplings, called doughboys, were made by frying bits of wet flour in pork fat. A real treat was burgoo—hot oatmeal and molasses. Another was plum duff. Duff was a fatty pudding. Plum duff had raisins or dried prunes mixed in.

Hot food was special. Aboard the *Mayflower,* nobody had it often. Usually the Pilgrims ate cold, dry, buggy meals, drank beer, and dreamed of how well they would eat when they finally reached America, the land of plenty. ●

Strategy Follow-up

Now complete the following concept map. List four foods described in "Bugs for Dinner."
Then write one or two descriptive details for each food, and tell which sense or senses it
appeals to. An example is shown.

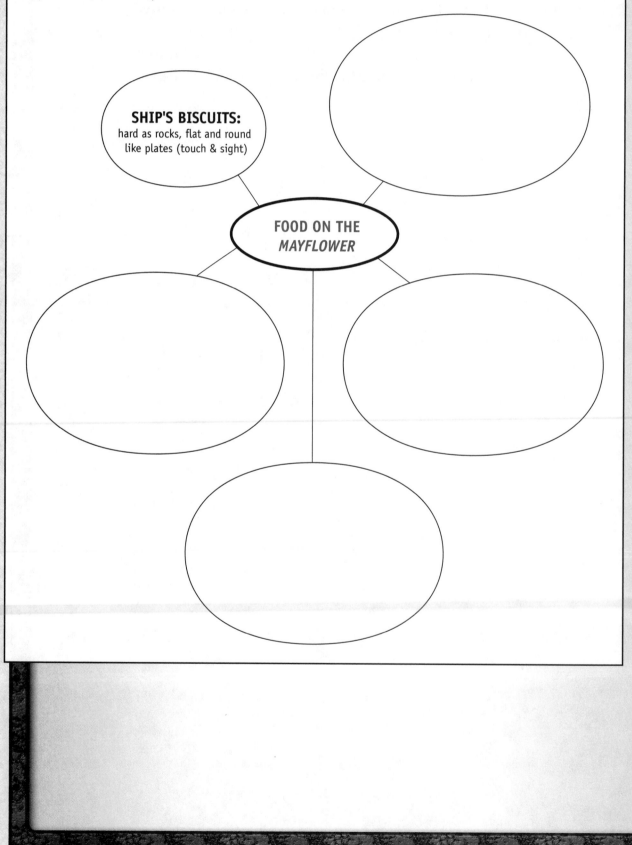

SHIP'S BISCUITS:
hard as rocks, flat and round
like plates (touch & sight)

FOOD ON THE
MAYFLOWER

✓Personal Checklist

Read each question and put a check (✓) in the correct box.

1. How well do you understand the hardships that the Pilgrims faced on their voyage to America?
   - ☐ 3 (extremely well)
   - ☐ 2 (fairly well)
   - ☐ 1 (not well)

2. How well could you tell someone else about the food described in this selection?
   - ☐ 3 (extremely well)
   - ☐ 2 (fairly well)
   - ☐ 1 (not well)

3. How well did the information in Building Background help you understand why the Pilgrims undertook the voyage?
   - ☐ 3 (extremely well)
   - ☐ 2 (fairly well)
   - ☐ 1 (not well)

4. How many sentences did you complete correctly in the Vocabulary Builder?
   - ☐ 3 (4–6 sentences)
   - ☐ 2 (2–3 sentences)
   - ☐ 1 (0–1 sentences)

5. How well were you able to complete the concept map in the Strategy Follow-up?
   - ☐ 3 (extremely well)
   - ☐ 2 (fairly well)
   - ☐ 1 (not well)

Vocabulary Check

Look back at the work you did in the Vocabulary Builder. Then answer each question by circling the correct letter.

1. A hot soup called labscouse was a treat for the Pilgrims because it tasted so good. Which vocabulary word best describes labscouse?
   - a. moldy
   - b. stale
   - c. delicious

2. The Pilgrims softened the ship's biscuits and then nibbled on them. What does *nibbled* mean?
   - a. bit off small pieces
   - b. took huge mouthfuls
   - c. fed to the mice

3. Which vocabulary word best describes meat that is packed in salt to make it last longer?
   - a. spoiled
   - b. preserved
   - c. delicious

4. How might you describe a hardened piece of bread?
   - a. stale
   - b. preserved
   - c. nibbled

5. What would you probably do with a piece of spoiled fruit today?
   - a. eat it
   - b. throw it away
   - c. preserve it

Add the numbers that you just checked to get your Personal Checklist score. Fill in your score here. Then turn to page 201 and transfer your score onto Graph 1.

Personal
Vocabulary
Strategy
Comprehension
TOTAL SCORE
✓ T

Check your answers with your teacher. Give yourself 1 point for each correct answer, and fill in your Vocabulary score here. Then turn to page 201 and transfer your score onto Graph 1.

Personal
Vocabulary
Strategy
Comprehension
TOTAL SCORE
✓ T

Strategy Check

Review the concept map that you completed in the Strategy Follow-up. Also review the rest of the selection. Then answer these questions:

1. The ship's biscuits were "stacked in huge piles." Which sense does this detail appeal to?

    a. smell

    b. sight

    c. sound

2. The vegetables were described as "a little hard on the outside and a little soft on the inside." Which sense does this detail appeal to?

    a. touch

    b. taste

    c. smell

3. The author describes the food that the Pilgrims ate as "cold, dry, and salty." Which two senses does this detail appeal to?

    a. sight and sound

    b. touch and taste

    c. smell and sound

4. Labscouse is described as thick, hot, and delicious. Which senses does this detail appeal to?

    a. smell, sound, and taste

    b. sound, sight, and taste

    c. sight, touch, and taste

5. Doughboys are described as "little fat dumplings." Which sense does this detail appeal to?

    a. smell

    b. sound

    c. sight

Comprehension Check

Review the selection if necessary. Then answer these questions:

1. Why didn't the Pilgrims eat the pigs, goats, and sheep that were on board?

    a. because they wanted to use the animals to start flocks and herds in America

    b. because the animals were kept in a rowboat lashed to the deck

    c. because the animals were covered with fleas and lice

2. Why did the Pilgrims need to drink a lot with their meals?

    a. because they never had enough food to eat

    b. because they used so many hot spices in their food

    c. because the dry, salty food made them thirsty

3. Why did some Pilgrims eat at night?

    a. so they wouldn't see the bugs on their food

    b. so they could cook a nice, hot dinner

    c. so the mice and rats wouldn't eat their food

4. What is burgoo?

    a. little fat dumplings

    b. pudding with raisins or prunes

    c. hot oatmeal and molasses

5. What did the Pilgrims look forward to as they ate their meals?

    a. returning to England

    b. arriving in America

    c. drinking fresh water

Check your answers with your teacher. Give yourself 1 point for each correct answer, and fill in your Strategy score here. Then turn to page 201 and transfer your score onto Graph 1.

Personal
Vocabulary
Strategy
Comprehension
TOTAL SCORE
✓ T

Check your answers with your teacher. Give yourself 1 point for each correct answer, and fill in your Comprehension score here. Then turn to page 201 and transfer your score onto Graph 1.

Personal
Vocabulary
Strategy
Comprehension
TOTAL SCORE
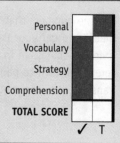
✓ T

Extending

Choose one or more of these activities:

DRAW A PICTURE OF THE *MAYFLOWER*

Draw a picture showing the outside of the *Mayflower*. Or use the descriptions in the selection to draw a picture of the ship's main cabin.

LEARN ABOUT THE PILGRIMS

Find out what happened to the Pilgrims after they reached America. Use the some of the resources on this page to help you answer these questions:

- How did the Pilgrims survive in America?

- What customs did they follow?

- What did they use to build their homes?

- How did the Pilgrims get along with Native Americans?

Present your findings in an oral report to your class.

COOK LIKE A PILGRIM

Find out what the Pilgrims ate once they settled in America. Use the books listed on this page for help if you need it. Prepare one of their favorite desserts, and share it with your class. Compare it to your own favorite sweets.

Resources

Books

Ames, Lee J. *Draw 50 Boats, Ships, Trucks and Trains.* Doubleday, 1987.

Erdosh, George. *Food and Recipes of the Pilgrims.* Cooking Throughout American History. Powerkids Press, 2001.

Penner, Lucille Recht. *Eating the Plates: A Pilgrim Book of Food and Manners.* Aladdin Paperbacks, 1997.

————. *The Pilgrims at Plymouth.* Random House, 1996.

Web Site

http://www.plimoth.org
This Web site lets you take a virtual tour of the Pilgrims' settlement in Massachusetts. It also contains links to pictures and information on the Pilgrims.

How the Mountain Gods Came to The People

Building Background

"How the Mountain Gods Came to The People" is an Apache tale. The Apache are Native Americans from the American Southwest. In this tale, the Apache are called "The People."

Like other Apache tales, "How the Mountain Gods Came to The People" has been passed down from generation to generation. Some Apache tales tell how the world began. Others tell about famous Apache warriors, such as Geronimo. Still others, like the tale you are about to read, teach lessons.

Think about the stories that are told in your family about you or other family members. Then get together with a partner and trade stories. Which one of your family stories would you like to have passed down from generation to generation?

disappeared

elderly

healed

huge

pure

sacrificed

solid

starve

tattered

unselfish

Vocabulary Builder

1. Each boldfaced vocabulary word on page 183 is followed by two other words or phrases. One of the two words or phrases is an antonym of the boldfaced word. (Reminder: **Antonyms** have opposite meanings.)

2. Before you begin reading the selection, circle the antonyms of any of the boldfaced words that you know. Then, as you read the selection, use context to help you figure out the other boldfaced words. Return to this exercise and circle the rest of the antonyms.

3. Save your work. You will use it again in the Vocabulary Check.

disappeared	vanished	showed up
elderly	old	young
healed	cured	injured
huge	very small	very big
pure	clean	dirty
sacrificed	kept something	gave something up
solid	soft	firm
starve	die from hunger	eat too much
tattered	whole	ragged
unselfish	generous	greedy

Strategy Builder

How to Read a Folktale

- "How the Mountain Gods Came to The People" is a folktale. A **folktale** is a simple story that has been passed from generation to generation by word of mouth. Folktales are usually told within particular families and cultures.

- Folktales tell different stories, but most have the same **elements**. Those elements include the following:

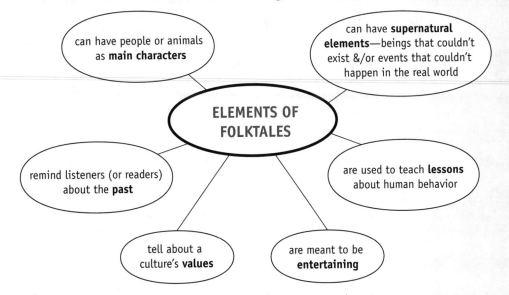

- As you read "How the Mountain Gods Came to The People," you will use a **concept map** to help you keep track of its folktale elements.

How the Mountain Gods Came to The People

by Claire R. Farrer

As you read the beginning of this selection, apply the strategies you just learned. See if you can find elements that make this story a folktale.

A very long time ago, a great sickness came on The People. The rains did not come to water the thirsty land. The People became hungry and ill. The wise people in the camp said they would have to move south, to where there was good water, plants, and animals, or they would **starve**.

The People packed up the camp. The very old and the babies were placed on horses; everyone else would walk. Everyone was ready to go except for two boys. One was blind, and the other was crippled. The two boys said that they would stay behind, for they knew that they would keep the others from moving quickly. When the two boys refused to change their minds, the others left them with heavy hearts.

Even though the boys were careful, the food and water that was left with them did not last long. One night, as they prepared to go to sleep, hungry and thirsty, dark clouds covered the moon and the stars in the sky. Suddenly, four **huge** men appeared in front of them. Their faces and bodies were covered with black except for a four-pointed star that glowed white. They wore headdresses and long kilts that reached almost to their ankles, and jingles sounded on their waists and ankles as they moved. Their moccasins were finely made and decorated.

⬣ **Stop here for the Strategy Break.**

Strategy Break

If you were to create a concept map of the folktale elements in this story so far, it might look like this:

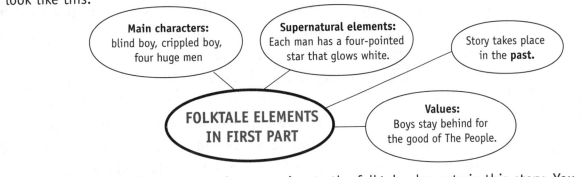

As you continue reading, keep paying attention to the folktale elements in this story. You will use them later in a concept map of your own.

Go on reading to see what happens.

A smaller figure, a clownish boy no bigger than the two boys, was walking behind the huge figures. The boy also was painted, although he did not wear a headdress and his kilt was short. Laughing, he gestured for the boys to follow him and the men. The four men and the boy walked up to the face of a mountain and **disappeared** inside. The head and shoulders of the boy reappeared, and again he gestured to the two boys to follow. Both boys closed their eyes, swallowed hard, and walked right through the **solid** rock as if it were water.

They followed the men and the boy until they found themselves in a cave deep inside the mountain. The two boys were offered water and food. They were given new clothes to replace their **tattered** ones. Each received a new pair of moccasins with jingles on them.

The men began to dance around a large fire in the middle of the cave-room. "We are the Mountain Gods," they said. "You were **unselfish** when you **sacrificed** yourselves so that your people could live. Watch us dance. Listen to the music. These are holy songs. They will help your people. Learn them."

Soon the two boys were singing and dancing with the Mountain Gods. They suddenly realized that the blind boy could see and the crippled boy was dancing without any pain or twisted limbs. Tired from dancing, they were shown places to sleep by the fire.

When they awakened, the fire had died and the cave was silent, but fresh food and water had been left for them. They put on their new clothes and moccasins.

In only four steps, the boys were back at their old camp. They began to follow the trail left by The People. In four days, they caught up with them. But the sentry did not recognize the boys, and a camp meeting was called so that The People could decide what to do with them.

As the once-blind boy began to talk, an **elderly** couple began to cry because his voice was exactly the same as that of the child they had left behind years ago. When the once-crippled boy began to speak, his voice was drowned out by the wailing of a very old woman who was convinced that she was hearing the voice of her son, whom she had not seen for years.

The boys were astonished. To their families and friends, years had passed since they had been left behind during the starving time! A young girl brought them a dipper of water. They saw the faces of grown men, not those of young boys, reflected in the water.

They related their story. They sang the songs they had been taught and demonstrated the dances of the Mountain Gods. They told The People that when they danced with **pure** hearts, the Mountain Gods would visit them in spirit and, through their dancing and singing, would cure all who needed help.

The boys told The People how to make the masks and headdresses, how to bless those who were to dance, and how to dance without tiring. The People followed the instructions. All were blessed, and those who were sick found comfort and were **healed**.

So the Apaches danced, and they still do. ●

Strategy Follow-up

On a separate sheet of paper, list the folktale elements in the second part of this story. Begin by adding the rest of the main characters. Then add the other supernatural events. Last, fill in the rest of the concept map.

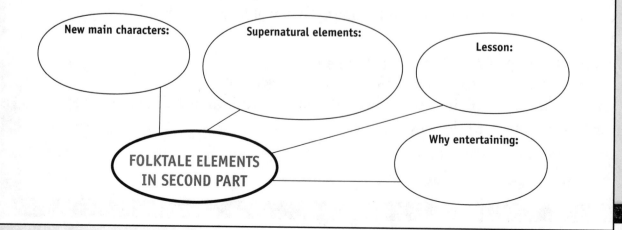

✓Personal Checklist

Read each question and put a check (✓) in the correct box.

1. How well do you understand the events in this Apache folktale?
   - ☐ 3 (extremely well)
   - ☐ 2 (fairly well)
   - ☐ 1 (not well)

2. How well do you understand why the Mountain Gods cured the two boys?
   - ☐ 3 (extremely well)
   - ☐ 2 (fairly well)
   - ☐ 1 (not well)

3. How well did the information and activity in Building Background help you understand why stories are passed down in families and cultures?
   - ☐ 3 (extremely well)
   - ☐ 2 (fairly well)
   - ☐ 1 (not well)

4. How many antonyms did you correctly circle in the Vocabulary Builder?
   - ☐ 3 (8–10 antonyms)
   - ☐ 2 (4–7 antonyms)
   - ☐ 1 (0–3 antonyms)

5. How well were you able to complete the concept map in the Strategy Follow-up?
   - ☐ 3 (extremely well)
   - ☐ 2 (fairly well)
   - ☐ 1 (not well)

Vocabulary Check

Look back at the work you did in the Vocabulary Builder. Then answer each question by circling the correct letter.

1. The two boys stayed behind so that they wouldn't slow down the others. Which vocabulary word best describes their behavior?
   - a. unselfish
   - b. tattered
   - c. disappeared

2. Which word is an antonym of *pure*?
   - a. dirty
   - b. clean
   - c. spotless

3. The Mountain Gods cured the two boys. What is an antonym of *cured*?
   - a. healed
   - b. treated
   - c. injured

4. Which word is an antonym of *elderly*?
   - a. old
   - b. sick
   - c. young

5. The Mountain Gods are giants. Which word best describes their size?
   - a. pure
   - b. huge
   - c. starved

Add the numbers that you just checked to get your Personal Checklist score. Fill in your score here. Then turn to page 201 and transfer your score onto Graph 1.

| | Personal |
| Vocabulary |
| Strategy |
| Comprehension |
| **TOTAL SCORE** |
✓ T

Check your answers with your teacher. Give yourself 1 point for each correct answer, and fill in your Vocabulary score here. Then turn to page 201 and transfer your score onto Graph 1.

| | Personal |
| Vocabulary |
| Strategy |
| Comprehension |
| **TOTAL SCORE** |
✓ T

Strategy Check

Review the concept map that you completed for the second part of this tale. Also review the rest of the tale. Then answer these questions:

1. The four men walked through the mountain. Which folktale element is this an example of?

    a. a character

    b. a lesson

    c. a supernatural event

2. Which character did you add to your concept map for the second part of this tale?

    a. the crippled boy

    b. the clownish boy

    c. the blind boy

3. Which of the following is a supernatural event?

    a. The guard did not recognize the boys when they came to the camp.

    b. The boys' mothers cried when they heard their sons' voices.

    c. Many years passed while the boys slept.

4. What lesson about human behavior does this folktale teach?

    a. Dancing will make you a better person.

    b. Unselfish behavior will be rewarded.

    c. Anyone can walk through solid rock.

5. Which of the following might you have listed to tell why the story is entertaining?

    a. I wanted to keep reading to find out what would happen next.

    b. I thought the story was long and boring.

    c. I didn't care what happened to the two boys.

Comprehension Check

Review the tale if necessary. Then answer these questions:

1. Why do The People decide to find a new home?

    a. They want to leave the two boys behind.

    b. They need to find a place with good water, plants, and animals.

    c. They are afraid of the Mountain Gods and what they will do.

2. How do the four men and the boys enter the mountain?

    a. They walk through it.

    b. They enter it through a cave.

    c. They dig their way into it.

3. What happens when the two boys begin dancing with the Mountain Gods?

    a. The boys receive new clothes.

    b. The boys both get healed.

    c. The boys walk through solid rock.

4. Why don't people in the camp recognize the boys?

    a. because the boys have become Mountain Gods

    b. because the boys have been healed

    c. because years have passed, and the boys are grown men

5. What is supposed to happen when The People dance with pure hearts?

    a. The Mountain Gods will make them grow older.

    b. The Mountain Gods will make them sick.

    c. The Mountain Gods will visit and cure them.

Check your answers with your teacher. Give yourself 1 point for each correct answer, and fill in your Strategy score here. Then turn to page 201 and transfer your score onto Graph 1.

Personal
Vocabulary
Strategy
Comprehension
TOTAL SCORE   ✓ T

Check your answers with your teacher. Give yourself 1 point for each correct answer, and fill in your Comprehension score here. Then turn to page 201 and transfer your score onto Graph 1.

Personal
Vocabulary
Strategy
Comprehension
TOTAL SCORE   ✓ T

Extending

Choose one or more of these activities:

WRITE A FOLKTALE

Write down a story that someone in your family tells. You might write the story that you shared in Building Background, or you might write a different one. The story can be about you or one of your family members. Try to choose a story that could become a folktale that is passed down to other generations in your family.

IDENTIFY FOLKTALE ELEMENTS IN OTHER TALES

Read another folktale. It could be another Apache tale or one from another culture. After you finish the story, use a concept map to list its folktale elements. If you need help finding a folktale, see the resources listed on this page.

DRAW THE MOUNTAIN GODS

Use the descriptions in this tale to help you draw the Mountain Gods. If necessary, do some research to find out what Apache headdresses, kilts, and moccasins look like. The resources on this page might help you get started. Then draw what the Mountain Gods looked like when they first appeared to the boys. Or draw what the Mountain Gods looked like as they danced.

Resources

Books

Hayes, Joe. *Coyote and Native American Folk Tales*. Mariposa Printing & Publishing, 1983.

Ronan, Christine, and Esther Grisham. *The Apache*. The Ancient and Living Cultures Series. Goodyear Publishing, 1998.

Sneve, Virginia Driving Hawk. *The Apaches*. Holiday House, 1997.

Sullivan, Charles. *American Folk: Classic Tales Retold*. Abrams Books for Young Readers, 1998.

Web Site

http://www.storiestogrowby.com
This site contain folktales and fairy tales from around the world.

Climbing the World's Highest Mountains

Building Background

The article you are about to read explains why people climb mountains. Some of the information will be new to you. But some of it may be information that you have already heard or read. Before you read this article, think of three things that you already know about mountain climbing. Then think of three questions that you have about it. As you read the article, look for answers to your questions.

altitude sickness

avalanche

blizzards

crevasse

glare

gusts

Vocabulary Builder

1. The words in the margin are all specialized vocabulary words. As you learned earlier in this book, **specialized vocabulary** words are related to a particular topic. For example, the words *ballast, launch, currents* and *expands* are all related to hot air ballooning.

2. Read the words and phrases below. The words in Column 1 are related to the hazards—or dangers—that mountain climbers face. Draw a line from each hazard in Column 1 to its definition in Column 2. (Use a dictionary if you need help.) Then think about how each hazard might endanger the life of a mountain climber.

3. Save your work. You will use it again in the Vocabulary Check.

COLUMN 1	COLUMN 2
altitude sickness	blinding snowstorms
avalanche	blasts or bursts of air
blizzards	condition caused by lack of oxygen
crevasse	brightness or brilliance
glare	deep, narrow crack in the ice
gusts	loose snow falling down a mountainside

Strategy Builder

Summarizing Main Ideas in Nonfiction

- As you know, **nonfiction** is writing that gives facts and information about a particular subject, or **topic**.

- When you read a long article or chapter on a topic, you're given much information at once. To keep the information straight—and to remember it better—it is helpful to stop once in a while and summarize. When you **summarize** a section of text, you list or retell in your own words just the **main ideas**, or most important points.

- Read the following paragraphs from an article on the Big Dipper. Think about how you might summarize the main ideas in these paragraphs.

The Big Dipper

The Big Dipper is a group of stars that many people see when they look into the northern sky. It is part of a larger group of stars called Ursa Major, or the Great Bear.

Some Native Americans see the bowl of the Big Dipper as a bear. They see the three stars in the handle as three warriors chasing the bear. Other people see the Big Dipper as everything from a cart to a plow to a bull's thigh—and even the Chinese government!

The Big Dipper had an important part in helping Southern slaves escape to freedom. The slaves thought that the Big Dipper looked like a ladle, or scoop, for drinking water. So they called the Big Dipper the "drinking gourd." They used the drinking gourd's North Star to find their way north to Canada—and freedom.

- How would you summarize these paragraphs in just a few sentences? Here is how one student did it:

The Big Dipper

- It's a group of stars found in Ursa Major (The Great Bear).

- People think it looks like different things.

- Slaves called it the "drinking gourd" and used its North Star to find their way to Canada.

Climbing the World's Highest Mountains

Look for the main ideas as you read this article. Stop from time to time and think about how you might summarize them.

Death is everywhere in these mountains. It lurks behind every gust of wind. It hides under every crack in the snow. Dozens of people have died here in the mountains of Asia. Yet climbers keep coming back. They come from around the world to take on peaks such as K2 and Everest.

Climbing small mountains is hard enough. You need strong ropes, special boots, and lots of courage. But climbing the world's highest mountains is even tougher. The higher you go, the thinner the air gets. By the time you reach 20,000 feet, your body can hardly function. There is barely enough oxygen in the air to keep you alive.

Most climbers carry small tanks of oxygen. But these tanks don't hold much. So parts of the climb must be done on your own. As your brain becomes starved for oxygen, you may find yourself getting dizzy and confused. Your nose might start to bleed. You might feel sick to your stomach. This **altitude sickness** is no joke. In 1993 a climber on K2 died from it.

Others, too, have struggled in the thin air. One was Andrzej Zawada. Zawada was a well-known climber. He had worked his way up many tall mountains. In 1980 he led a group up Mount Everest. At 29,028 feet, it is the highest peak in the world. The climb was a success. But it wasn't easy. "I felt the lack of oxygen very much." Zawada wrote.

Zawada's group also had to deal with bad weather. That is a classic problem on these mountains. Temperatures often drop far below zero. Zawada's men were hit by bitterly cold air. At one point, it was forty degrees below zero *inside their tent!*

Sometimes things warm up a bit. Even so, **blizzards** can move in quickly. K2, the worlds' second highest mountain, is famous for its storms. They can last for days. They can bury climbers in several feet of new snow. In 1986, five people died when they were trapped in this kind of storm on K2.

Each snowfall brings yet another hazard. The weight of new snow can cause an **avalanche**. If you're caught in an avalanche on Everest or one of the other big mountains, there's not much you can do. Just the thought of being caught in an avalanche makes climbers shiver with fear.

Scott Fischer almost died that way. In 1992 he and Ed Viesturs were climbing K2. Suddenly, huge chunks of snow crashed down on them.

Fischer was swept down the mountain. Viesturs, who was roped to him, also began to fall. Luckily, Viesturs managed to dig his ice ax into the ground. The two men came to a stop at the edge of a 4,000-foot cliff.

Winds also post a threat. They may whip past at one hundred miles per hour. In 1995 Alison Hargreaves fell victim to these winds. Hargreaves was one of the best climbers in the world. She was the first woman ever to reach the top of Mount Everest alone and without an oxygen tank. Only one other person had ever done this before.

On August 13, 1995, Hargreaves was on K2. Winds were high. Late that day, she and five other climbers struggled to the top of the mountain. They started back down again. But the winds grew worse, slowing the group's progress. All night, fierce **gusts** swirled around the mountain. Hargreaves and the others kept going. They tried to get back to their campsite. But they never made it. It appears that sometime during this frightful night, they were swept off their feet. They were literally blown to their deaths. Hargreaves's body was later found in an icy nook not far from camp.

⬣ **Stop here for the Strategy Break.**

Strategy Break

Did you stop and summarize as you read? If you did, see if your summaries match these:

- Dozens of people have died while climbing mountains.

- Climbing small mountains is hard, but climbing the world's highest ones is even harder.

- The higher you go, the thinner the air gets. If you don't have enough oxygen, you can get altitude sickness—and possibly die.

- Bad weather is a problem. Temperatures often drop far below zero. Blizzards can move in quickly and last for days.

- The weight of new snow can cause an avalanche.

- Winds also pose a threat. They can whip past at 100 mph.

 Go on reading.

And then there is the danger of falling into a **crevasse**. A crevasse is a narrow crack in the ice. It may be hundreds of feet deep. If there is a little fresh snow covering it, you may not see it until it's too late. Scott Fischer once fell into a crevasse. He didn't fall far, but his body became jammed in the crack. He was locked between two walls of ice. When another climber pulled him out, Fischer found that his right arm had been twisted out of its socket.

The list of dangers goes on and on. Mountain climbers can be blinded by the **glare** of sunlight reflecting off the snow. That happened to Peggy Luce. The year was 1988. Luce was trying to become the second American woman ever to reach the top of Mount Everest. Her goggles became foggy on the way up. She took them off and kept climbing. Luce made it to the top. But as she came back down, she had trouble seeing. She realized she was suffering from snow blindness. People usually recover from this, but it takes a while. Luce knew she had to keep going. She had to get out of the sun and rest her eyes. She stumbled on down the mountain. At one point, she bent over to see where she was putting her foot. She lost her balance. She began to roll down the mountain. Luckily, she dug her ice ax into the snow, stopping her fall. Luce made it to safety. But the next day, her eyes were swollen shut.

Sometimes climbers simply run out of energy. Then they might collapse in the snow and wait for death to come. Perhaps that's what happened to a German woman who died on Everest in the 1970s. She was later found, frozen in a sitting position with her head on her knees. "She made it to the top, but she didn't get down," concluded climber David Breashears.

Given all the hardships, why do people choose this sport? What makes them run such terrible risks? Many climbers have tried to explain it. Andrzej Zawada said he wanted to "conquer" the highest peaks. Roger Mear said that to succeed when "chances are limited—that's what mountaineering is all about." Giusto Gervasutti called mountain climbing "an inner need." He said it showed "the freedom of the [human] spirit." But perhaps Alison Hargreaves explained it best. Hargreaves knew that someday she might die on a mountain. But as she put it, "One day as a tiger is better than a thousand as a sheep." ●

Strategy Follow-up

First think about your questions from Building Background. Did you find their answers?
  Next, use a separate sheet of paper to write a summary for the second part of this article. Be sure to list only the most important ideas. Skip unnecessary details.

✓Personal Checklist

Read each question and put a check (✓) in the correct box.

1. In Building Background, how well were you able to think of three questions about mountain climbing?
    - ☐ 3   (extremely well)
    - ☐ 2   (fairly well)
    - ☐ 1   (not well)

2. In the Vocabulary Builder, how well were you able to match the vocabulary words and their definitions?
    - ☐ 3   (extremely well)
    - ☐ 2   (fairly well)
    - ☐ 1   (not well)

3. In the Strategy Follow-up, how well were you able to summarize the second part of the article?
    - ☐ 3   (extremely well)
    - ☐ 2   (fairly well)
    - ☐ 1   (not well)

4. How well do you understand the hazards of mountain climbing?
    - ☐ 3   (extremely well)
    - ☐ 2   (fairly well)
    - ☐ 1   (not well)

5. How well do you understand why people climb mountains in spite of the hazards?
    - ☐ 3   (extremely well)
    - ☐ 2   (fairly well)
    - ☐ 1   (not well)

Vocabulary Check

Look back at the work you did in the Vocabulary Builder. Then answer each question by circling the correct letter.

1. What condition is caused by a lack of oxygen?
    - a. avalanche
    - b. snow blindness
    - c. altitude sickness

2. Which vocabulary word describes the cause of snow blindness?
    - a. gusts
    - b. glare
    - c. crevasse

3. People think that strong gusts on K2 blew Alison Hargreaves to her death. What are gusts?
    - a. deep cracks in the ice
    - b. strong blasts of wind
    - c. blinding snowstorms

4. What happens during an avalanche?
    - a. loose snow falls quickly down a mountain
    - b. strong winds swirl around a mountain
    - c. several feet of blinding snow fall from the sky

5. How long can some blizzards last?
    - a. several seconds
    - b. several days
    - c. several weeks

Add the numbers that you just checked to get your Personal Checklist score. Fill in your score here. Then turn to page 201 and transfer your score onto Graph 1.

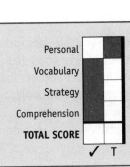

Check your answers with your teacher. Give yourself 1 point for each correct answer, and fill in your Vocabulary score here. Then turn to page 201 and transfer your score onto Graph 1.

Strategy Check

Look back at your summary for the second part of this article. Then answer these questions:

1. Which sentence does *not* summarize one of this article's main ideas?

   a. Hargreaves and the others kept going.

   b. Climbers can be blinded by the sun's glare.

   c. Sometimes climbers simply run out of energy.

2. Which sentence *does* summarize one of this article's main ideas?

   a. He didn't fall far, but his body became jammed in the crack.

   b. Luckily, she dug her ice ax into the snow, stopping her fall.

   c. Falling into a crevasse is dangerous because it can be hundreds of feet deep.

3. Which phrase best states the topic of this article?

   a. mountain climbing

   b. altitude sickness

   c. mountain climbers

4. Name two of the hazards, or dangers, described in the second part of this article.

   a. getting caught in a blizzard and getting snow blindness

   b. falling into a crevasse and running out of energy

   c. getting altitude sickness and getting hit by gusts of wind

5. Which sentence best summarizes this entire article?

   a. As your brain becomes starved for oxygen, you may find yourself getting dizzy.

   b. K2, the world's second highest mountain, is famous for its storms.

   c. Given the many dangers, people still think it's worth it to climb mountains.

Comprehension Check

Review the article if necessary. Then answer these questions:

1. Why does it appear that Alison Hargreaves was "swept off her feet"?

   a. She fell in love on K2.

   b. She fell into a crevasse on K2.

   c. Her body was found near her camp.

2. Which mountain is famous for its storms?

   a. K2

   b. Everest

   c. McKinley

3. Why are avalanches a hazard to mountain climbers?

   a. because their movement causes an earthquake

   b. because their movement causes a volcano

   c. because climbers can get buried under the falling snow

4. What is *not* one of the possible symptoms of altitude sickness?

   a. Your nose might start to bleed.

   b. You are blinded from the glare of the sun.

   c. You could get dizzy and confused.

5. Which quote sums up why some people climb mountains?

   a. "I felt the lack of oxygen very much."

   b. "One day as a tiger is better than a thousand as a sheep."

   c. "She made it to the top, but she didn't get down."

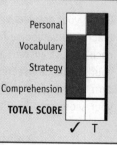

Check your answers with your teacher. Give yourself 1 point for each correct answer, and fill in your Strategy score here. Then turn to page 201 and transfer your score onto Graph 1.

Personal
Vocabulary
Strategy
Comprehension
TOTAL SCORE
✓ T

Check your answers with your teacher. Give yourself 1 point for each correct answer, and fill in your Comprehension score here. Then turn to page 201 and transfer your score onto Graph 1.

Personal
Vocabulary
Strategy
Comprehension
TOTAL SCORE
✓ T

Extending

Choose one or more of these activities:

REPORT ON AVALANCHES

Find out what causes avalanches and how to stay as safe as possible during an avalanche. Use the resources listed on this page for help, or find ones of your own. Present your findings in an oral report. If possible, use photos in your presentation.

MAKE A CATALOG

Make a short catalog of some of the equipment and clothing available to today's mountaineers. The Web sites listed on this page will give you a place to start. Or you can talk to someone at your local sporting goods store. Include your own drawing or photo with the description of each item. Also tell what the item is for and how it is useful.

CREATE A BROCHURE

Using the resources listed on this page or ones you find yourself, create a brochure of safety tips for mountain climbers. You might want to present the information in lists—for example: The Top Ten Pieces of Safety Equipment that Every Mountaineer Should Own.

MAKE "STAT SHEETS"

Research the five highest mountains in the world and highlight their locations on a map or globe. (The article mentions two of them.) Then write a "stat sheet" for each mountain that includes the following information:

- the country or state in which the mountain is located

- its height in both feet and meters

- the name of the first person (or people) to reach its summit

- one or two interesting or unusual facts about it

Resources

Books

Kocour, Ruth Anne, with Michael Hodgson. *Facing the Extreme: One Woman's Story of True Courage, Death-Defying Survival, and Her Quest for the Summit.* St. Martin's Press, 1998.

Tilton, Buck. *Basic Essentials of Avalanche Safety.* ICS Books, 1992.

Web Sites

http://www.adventurenetwork.com/CLIMBTemp.html
This site includes links to fitness and training, first aid and safety, and clothing and fabrics for mountain climbers. It also has a bookstore.

http://www.gorp.com/gorp/gear/main.htm
This Web site give mountaineers information on how to pack, what to wear, and what gear to use.

http://www.teacher.scholastic.com/hillary/archive/toptenmt.htm
This site lists the ten most famous mountains, gives their location and height, and tells when they were first climbed.

Video/DVD

Everest. Miramax Home Entertainment, 1998.

Learning New Words

VOCABULARY

From Lesson 16
- cones
- pupil
- rods

From Lesson 20
- glare

Multiple-Meaning Words

As you know, a single word can have more than one meaning. For example, the word *glare* can mean "a very bright light" or "a bright, smooth surface" or "an angry stare." To figure out which meaning of *glare* an author is using, you have to use context. Context is the information surrounding a word or situation that helps you understand its meaning.

When you read "Climbing the World's Highest Mountains," you used context to figure out that the author uses *glare* to mean "the very bright light" of the sun.

Use context to figure out the correct meaning of each underlined word. Circle the letter of the correct meaning.

1. We like to eat our ice cream in waffle <u>cones</u>.

   a. seeds from a pine tree

   b. baked dough containers

2. Our new curtain <u>rods</u> look great above the living room windows.

   a. thin, straight bars of metal or wood

   b. units of length equaling 5.5 yards

3. Jack's <u>pupil</u> got smaller when the doctor shined a light on it.

   a. part of the eye

   b. part of a classroom

4. Caterpillars go through a several <u>stages</u> before they become butterflies.

   a. platforms on which actors perform

   b. steps of development

5. We took a ferry across the <u>sound</u> to get to Seattle.

   a. narrow body of water

   b. thing that can be heard

Prefixes

A prefix is a word part that is added to the beginning of a root word. When you add a prefix, you often change the root word's meaning and function. For example, the prefix *pre-* means "before." So adding *pre-* to *heat* changes the word *heat* to the verb *preheat,* which means "heat before using or eating."

in-

The prefix *in-* means "not" or "the opposite of." The word *visible* means "seen." Adding the prefix *in-* to *visible* changes the word to its antonym, which means "not visible."

Write the word that describes each definition below.

1. not capable   _____

2. the opposite of active   _____

3. not complete   _____

4. the opposite of equality   _____

Suffixes

A suffix is a word part that is added to the end of a root word. When you add a suffix, you often change the root word's meaning and function. For example, the suffix *-less* means "without," so the root word *pain* changes from a noun to the adjective *painless,* meaning "without pain."

-ful

The suffix *-ful* means "full of _____" or "showing _____." In Lesson 17 you learned that photographer Jodi Cobb tries to show people a respectful attitude. *Respectful* means "full of respect."

Write the word that describes each definition below.

1. full of fear   _____

2. full of joy   _____

3. showing care   _____

4. showing grace   _____

VOCABULARY

From Lesson 17
• invisible

From Lesson 17
• respectful

Graphing Your Progress

The graphs on page 201 will help you track your progress as you work through this book. Follow these directions to fill in the graphs:

Graph 1

1. Start by looking across the top of the graph for the number of the lesson you just finished.

2. In the first column for that lesson, write your Personal Checklist score in both the top and bottom boxes. (Notice the places where *13* is filled in on the sample.)

3. In the second column for that lesson, fill in your scores for the Vocabulary, Strategy, and Comprehension Checks.

4. Add the three scores, and write their total in the box above the letter *T*. (The *T* stands for "Total." The ✓ stands for "Personal Checklist.")

5. Compare your scores. Does your Personal Checklist score match or come close to your total scores for that lesson? Why or why not?

Graph 2

1. Again, start by looking across the top of the graph for the number of the lesson you just finished.

2. In the first column for that lesson, shade the number of squares that match your Personal Checklist score.

3. In the second column for that lesson, shade the number of squares that match your total score.

4. As you fill in this graph, you will be able to check your progress across the book. You'll be able to see your strengths and areas of improvement. You'll also be able to see areas where you might need a little extra help. You and your teacher can discuss ways to work on those areas.

Graph 1

For each lesson, enter the scores from your Personal Checklist and your Vocabulary, Strategy, and Comprehension Checks. Total your scores and then compare them. Does your Personal Checklist score match or come close to your total scores for that lesson? Why or why not?

Go down to Graph 2 and shade your scores for the lesson you just completed.

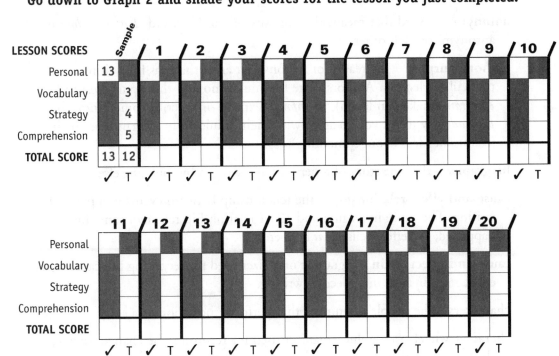

Graph 2

Now record your overall progress. In the first column for the lesson you just completed, shade the number of squares that match your Personal Checklist score. In the second column for that lesson, shade the number of squares that match your total score. As you fill in this graph, you will be able to check your progress across the book.

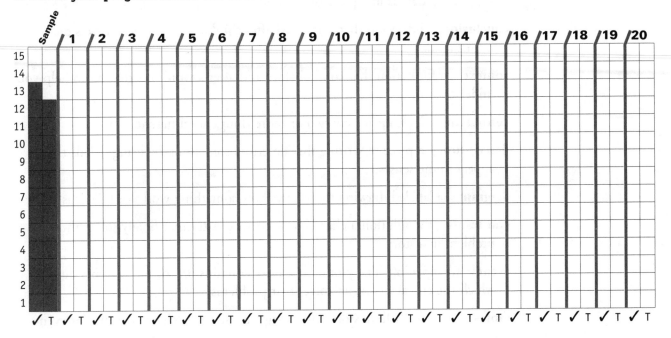

Glossary of Terms

This glossary includes definitions for important terms introduced in this book.

antonym   a word that means the opposite of another word. *Fast* and *slow* are antonyms of each other.

author's purpose   the reason or reasons that an author has for writing a particular selection. Authors write for one or more of these purposes: to *entertain* (make you laugh), to *inform* (explain or describe something), to *persuade* (try to get you to agree with their opinion), to *express* (share their feelings or ideas about something).

biography   the true story of a person's life, written by someone else.

cause-and-effect relationship   the relationship between events in a piece of writing. The cause in a cause-and-effect relationship tells *why* something happened; the effect tells *what* happened.

cause-and-effect chain   a graphic organizer used for recording the cause-and-effect relationships in a piece of writing.

characters   the people or animals that perform the action in a story.

character wheel   a graphic organizer used for recording the changes that a character goes through from the beginning to the end of a story.

comparing   looking at how two or more things are alike.

comparison chart   a graphic organizer used for showing how two or more people, places, things, or events are alike and different.

compound word   a word that is made up of two words put together. *Sundial* and *weekend* are examples of compound words.

concept map   a graphic organizer used for recording the main ideas and supporting details in a piece of writing.

conclusion   a decision that is reached after thinking about certain facts or information.

context   information that comes before and after a word or situation to help you understand it.

contrasting   looking at how two or more things are different.

description   a piece of writing that describes something by using details that appeal to the senses.

diagram   a labeled drawing that shows how something works or how it is made.

end result   the solution a character or characters try that finally solves the problem in a story.

event   a happening. The plot of any story contains one or more events during which the characters try to solve their problems.

fantasy   a make-believe story with imaginary settings, characters, and/or events.

fiction   stories about made-up characters or events. Forms of fiction include short stories, historical fiction, fantasy, and folktales.

first person point of view   the perspective, or viewpoint, of one of the characters in a story. That character uses words such as *I, me, my,* and *mine* to tell the story.

folktale   a story that has been passed from generation to generation by word of mouth.

graphic organizer   a chart, graph, or drawing used to show how the main ideas in a piece of writing are organized and related.

headings   the short titles given throughout a piece of nonfiction. The headings often state the main ideas of a selection.

historical fiction   a made-up story based on real historical facts or events.

informational article   a piece of writing that gives facts and details about a particular subject, or topic.

interview   a piece of writing that records the questions and answers given during a conversation.

interviewer   the person asking the questions during an interview, or conversation.

main idea   the most important idea of a paragraph, section, or whole piece of writing.

multiple-meaning word   a word that has more than one meaning. The word *glare* is a multiple-meaning word whose meanings include "a very bright light," "a bright, smooth surface," and "an angry stare."

mystery   a story that contains a kind of puzzle that the characters must solve.

narrator   the person or character who is telling a story.

nonfiction   writing that gives facts and information about real people, events, and topics. Informational articles and biographies are some forms of nonfiction.

plot   the sequence of events in a piece of writing.

point of view   the perspective, or viewpoint, from which a story is told.

prediction   a kind of guess that is based on the context clues given in a story.

prefix   a word part that is added to the beginning of a root word. When you add a prefix, you often change the word's meaning and function. For example, the prefix *pre-* means "before." So adding *pre-* to *heat* changes the verb *heat* to the verb *preheat,* which means "heat before using or eating."

problem   difficulty or question that a character must solve or answer.

problem-solution frame   a graphic organizer used for recording the problem, solutions, and end result in a piece of writing.

sequence   the order of events in a piece of writing. The sequence shows what happens or what to do first, second, and so on.

sequence chain   a graphic organizer used for recording the sequence of events in a piece of writing. Sequence chains are used mostly for shorter periods of time, and time lines are used mostly for longer periods of time.

setting   the time and place in which a story happens.

signal words   words and phrases that tell when something happens or when to do something. Examples of signal words are *first, next, then, finally, after lunch,* and *two years later.*

solution   the things that characters or people do to solve a problem.

specialized vocabulary   words that are related to a particular subject, or topic. Specialized vocabulary words in the selection "Hot Air Ballooning" include *ballast, currents,* and *launch.*

story map   a graphic organizer used for recording the main parts of a story: its title, setting, character, problem, events, and solution.

suffix   a word part that is added to the end of a word. Adding a suffix usually changes the word's meaning and function. For example, the suffix *-less* means "without." So the word *pain* changes from a noun to the adjective *painless,* which means "without pain."

summary   a short description. A summary describes what has happened so far in a piece of fiction, or what the main ideas are in a piece of nonfiction.

supporting details   details that describe or explain the main idea of a paragraph, section, or whole piece of text.

symbol   a word, idea, picture, or object that represents, or stands for, something else. A heart is a common symbol for love.

synonym   a word that has the same meaning as another word. *Fast* and *quick* are synonyms of each other.

time line   a graphic organizer used for recording the sequence of events in a piece of writing. Time lines are used mostly for longer periods of time, and sequence chains are used mostly for shorter periods of time.

title   the name of a piece of writing.

topic   the subject of a piece of writing. The topic is what the selection is all about.

Acknowledgments

Acknowledgment is gratefully made to the following publishers, authors, and agents for permission to reprint these works. Every effort has been made to determine copyright owners. In the case of any omissions, the Publisher will be pleased to make suitable acknowledgments in future editions.

"Bamboo Can Do" from *Contemporary Reader*, Vol. 2, No. 1. Copyright 1998 by Jamestown Publishers, a division of NTC/Contemporary Publishing Group.

The *Big Balloon Race* by Eleanor Coerr. Text copyright © 1981 by Eleanor Coerr. Used by permission of HarperCollins Publishers.

From *Bridges* by Graham Rickard. Copyright © 1986 Wayland Publishers Ltd. Reprinted by permission of the publisher.

"Bugs for Dinner" reprinted with the permission of Simon & Schuster Books for Young Readers, an imprint of Simon & Schuster Children's Publishing Division from *Eating the Plates* by Lucille Recht Penner. Copyright © 1991 Lucille Recht Penner.

"Building Bridges" by Julie Tozier, *Highlights*, December 1997, Vol. 52, No. 12, Issue 554. Copyright © 1997 by Highlights for Children, Inc., Columbus, Ohio. Reprinted by permission.

"Climbing the World's Highest Mountain" from *The Wild Side: Extreme Sports*. Copyright 1996 by Jamestown Publishers, Inc., a division of NTC/Contemporary Publishing Group, Inc.

"ColorBlind" by Jane Scherer, from *Children's Digest*, copyright © 1991 by Children's Better Health Institute, Benjamin Franklin Literary & Medical Society, Inc., Indianapolis, Indiana. Used by permission.

"Derby" by Michael O. Tunnell. Reprinted by permission of *Cricket* magazine, June 1994, Vol. 21, No. 10. Copyright © 1994 by Michael O. Tunnell.

"Electric Cars" from *Contemporary Reader*, Vol. 1, No. 2. Copyright 1996 by Jamestown Publishers, a division of Contemporary Books, Inc.

From *Hot Air Ballooning* by Christie Costanzo. Copyright © 1991 by Capstone Press, Inc. Reprinted by permission of the publisher.

"How the Mountain Gods Came to the People, An Apache Tale" by Claire R. Farrer. Reprinted by permission of Claire R. Farrer; from a story by the same name first published in 1996 in *Cobblestone* Magazine.

"Just a Girl" by Brenda S. Cox, as appeared in *Hopscotch*, Vol. 10, No. 1, June/July 1998. Copyright © 1995 by Brenda S. Cox. Reprinted by permission of the author.

From *L. Frank Baum* by Carol Greene. Copyright © 1995 by Childrens Press®, Inc. Reprinted by permission of Grolier Publishing.

"Listen to the Drumbeat" by Nanette Larsen Dunford from *Children's Digest*, copyright © 1991 by Children's Better Health Institute, Benjamin Franklin Literary & Medical Society, Inc., Indianapolis, Indiana. Used by permission.

"The Mystery in the Attic" by Jeanne B. Hargett, *Highlights*, December 1997, Vol. 52, No. 12, Issue 554. Copyright © 1997 by Highlights for Children, Inc., Columbus, Ohio. Reprinted by permission.

"The Mystery of the Scythe" by Mat Rapacz. Reprinted by permission of *Cricket* magazine, February 1996, Vol. 23, No. 6. Copyright © 1996 by Mat Rapacz.

"Picturing the World: The Adventures of a Professional Photographer" by Allison Lassieur, *Highlights*, April 1997, Vol. 52, No. 4, Issue 546. Copyright © 1997 by Highlights for Children, Inc., Columbus, Ohio. Reprinted by permission.